TIGIST

TIGIST

THE FURY OF A PATIENT FATHER

A MEMOIR

ZAVIAN ESCANDAR

authorHOUSE®

AuthorHouse™
1663 Liberty Drive
Bloomington, IN 47403
www.authorhouse.com
Phone: 1-800-839-8640

Published by AuthorHouse   10/17/2014

ISBN: 978-1-4969-4060-5 (sc)
ISBN: 978-1-4969-4061-2 (e)

Library of Congress Control Number: 2014916777

This book is dedicated to my two lovely daughters.
Your patience, bravery, unconditional love and faith kept me going.

To the many friends and family members who stood by me.

To the abundant grace of God
May everyone's faith in Him be strengthened or restored.

Special thanks to my attorney, John Tasker, and
his brilliant assistant, Lynn Johnson

"Beware the fury of a patient man"

—John Dryden

It would be better for him if a millstone were hung around his neck and he were cast into the sea than that he should cause one of these little ones to sin.

Luke 17:2

If then, you being evil, know how to give good gifts to your children, how much more shall your father who is in heaven give what is good to those who ask him?

Matthew 7:11

Where do I begin, my buddy? You used to love it when I called you "buddy." I would talk with my friends on the phone while you were next to me and I would refer to them as buddies. So one day I said to you, "How are you doing there, Buddy?" and your face lit up. You loved hearing that and I continued to use that with you for a while. And as you were growing up, you called me "Bob," short for "Baba," and I, too, enjoyed hearing that.

It's late in the evening and I'm thinking about you and your sister. I miss you both terribly. You are the best thing that has ever happened for me, and here you are thousands of miles away. I'm counting the days to when I will, hopefully, see you again. It's been almost two years since your mother took you both away from me and broke up our family. Needless to say, it has been the most difficult thing I've ever had to go through. And something I would not wish upon my worst enemy. I'm so sorry that you're going through this and I promise that I will do everything in my power for us to reunite again.

What your mother did was morally wrong and you will realize this as you get older.

We had what most people would consider, "the perfect life here in America." We had a nice house located in a beautiful lakeside community, and God had blessed us with two loving and healthy children. I had a beautiful wife, a successful career that provided us with a comfortable lifestyle, and we were surrounded with family, friends and relatives who loved us. You went to a nice school and had many good friends. I could not have asked for more. But all of that would come to a sudden end when your mother decided to take you and your sister to Syria on an alleged two month vacation. Against my better judgment, I agreed to it.

As I begin to share with you this story and the events that took place soon after you left for Syria, my heart goes out to you and your sister. While some of the information I will share with you may, at times, be hurtful or even embarrassing, I want to assure you that I am not doing it to be spiteful or vindictive towards your mother or anyone else. I am simply sharing with you my personal feelings and struggles, with the hope that you and your sister will have a better understanding of our lives and forgive your parents for this very difficult situation we put you through. I think you have the right to know how all of this transpired and what led to this horrible outcome.

You left for Syria on June 28, 2010, and were to be back by the 6th of September so you could start school on the 7th.

About two years prior to your departure to Syria, your mother and I began to grow apart. She became more distant from me and withdrawn from our life as a family. We had a very hard time trying to communicate with one another. This was nothing new, as we had always had disagreements throughout our marriage. As a matter of fact, it had been that way from the very beginning. However, the last two years, in particular, were by far the most troubling.

Your mother and I were married on October 14, 2001, in Syria while I was vacationing there with my mother. Things were different then; I was different. I had turned thirty-four years of age that year and, in my mind, I was ready to find the woman I would spend the rest of my life with. People always told me that I did not look my age, that I looked ten years younger. I had had a good life thus far and prided myself as being a successful man in many ways. That is not to say I was rich financially, but that I had experienced the taste of success with the many business ventures and crazy ideas I had come up with in the hopes of someday becoming a millionaire.

After many attempts at success, and practically depleting my life savings on the many failed ideas, I took a few months off to assess my life and where I was headed. I needed an income to sustain my way of life and found myself applying for a job at a local car dealership. At first it was hard for me to be working for someone, as I had always had my own business, but I got used to it and found that I was good at this car selling gig – and the money was not bad, either. I liked this job and soon set my sights on moving up in the company.

A few months after I began my new career, I decided to go on vacation to Syria with my mother. For starters I would take some time off to see Syria for the first time since we moved to America over twenty years earlier, and also, as my mother said, "You might find someone there to share your new life with." This was very normal for men to go back to their native land and find a bride. And so it was, in August 2001, we were on our way to Syria.

I must say that I truly enjoyed that trip. We stayed at my sister's house in Alfouhila, a small town on the outskirts of Homs, which is one of the largest cities in Syria. That is where I was born, but it had changed so much from the vague memories I had in my head. I walked around the town trying to see where I used to play in order to trigger some suppressed memories. It seemed that I had no memories of my childhood at all. Most of what I remember was after the age of ten. What ever happened to the early years?

I began to trace my steps from the house I used to live in to the schools I attended. Nothing was bringing back the slightest recollection. Nonetheless, I met so many nice people there and visited with old friends who had to reintroduce themselves to me.

After a week of receiving guests, cousins, and family members, my mother started to push the idea of meeting someone whom I might call my wife. My sister suggested that I go to a relative's wedding party in a town called Alhafar. She said that there might be some girls there I might like. It was there that I saw your mother for the first time. I noticed her from a distance and thought that she might be a girl I would consider.

So I asked about her. I was told that her name was Dania, that she was a great girl from a good family and that her mother was a distant cousin of my father. As the night was coming to an end, she walked by our table and our eyes met for a few seconds. I was sitting with some friends and one of them asked her to come over. They introduced us and a moment later she went on her way. They asked me what I thought of her, and I said that she was very pretty, but a little too tall for me.

As my vacation was coming to an end, I had accepted the fact that I did not find anyone in Syria I could call my wife. And so I would spend the next few days just relaxing and enjoying my vacation. My mother, on the other hand, was not very happy. She was hoping that I would find a girl so that she might finally relax and have some peace, with all of her children now married.

Our departing flight back to America was scheduled for the 15th of September. The 11th of September of that year would change everything. I went to bed the night before just like any other night. When I woke up that morning and saw what had taken place in America, and the images that appeared on the screen of the twin towers on fire, I was in shock. I could not fathom what was happening. I wanted to be back in America. I told my mother what had happened and she was heartbroken. It felt surreal as these images were being played and replayed a hundred times. America was under attack.

We received the news that all flights into and out of the United States were now suspended till further notice. I called my travel agent to confirm our flight and was told to postpone the flight for two weeks or until further notice. For the next week or so we were glued to the television and had no interest in doing anything else.

Later on the morning of the 11th, my sister and I were having breakfast and she asked if I had seen any girls at the wedding party that I would consider.

"Yes," I replied, "I did meet one girl. Her name is Dania and she is very pretty, but I don't think she's for me."

My sister said that she knew the girl and her family well and asked me if she could call the girl's mother to see if they would receive us for a cup of coffee. After sharing with her my reservations regarding that, she assured me that it would not be a formal visit. She said that we would just have some coffee with some distant cousins and, if I felt anything towards Dania, then it would be up to me at that point. I agreed.

We went to meet the girl and her family in the city of Homs where they also had a home. They received us with a warm greeting and we had a chance to talk and share information about my life in America and her life in Syria. After visiting for an hour or so, I thanked them for their hospitality and my sister and I went back to Alfouhila.

I told my sister that I would call the girl again and ask if she would like to have lunch with me and then see where it might lead. After a couple of dates with your mother, I asked her to be my wife. A couple of weeks later, we were married. We went on a short, three day honeymoon to Latakia, a city in Syria set on the Mediterranean Sea.

After the honeymoon, I then made my way back to America alone and began the paperwork process to have your mother join me. About three months later she arrived in America to begin our life together.

Chapter 1

Early in 2002 your mother arrived in America after receiving all of the proper documents, and I went to the airport to pick her up, along with a few members of my family. The first week was a little difficult for both of us. The idea that I had gone to another country and gotten married was still a blur for me. I shared with your mother my feelings and suggested, because we did not have ample time in Syria to really get to know each other and to have the normal courting period newlyweds generally had, that it would make sense for us to take our time and not jump into the obligations of marriage right away.

I suggested that to make her – and me – more comfortable with one another. She took it the wrong way and thought that I perhaps had had a change of heart about being married to her. But, in reality, it had been a few months since we'd been together – and then only for a short time – and I really did not know her as well as I wanted to. We sort of rushed our marriage due to the time restraint I had been under in Syria.

That first week would almost set the tone for what was to come. Perhaps I was a little insensitive or naïve about her feelings about being away from her family and meeting new people and being in a different culture. But she showed me a side of her that I didn't particularly like. She was trying to adjust to her new life away from her family. I understood, for the most part, that she was new here and that she needed time, but she was taking out her frustration on me.

It took all of my patience to put up with her many mood swings. It was a constant struggle for her to fit in with the family. Since I had been single for so long, I had developed a tight relationship with every member of my family, and she said she felt like she was sharing me and my time with them. This created friction and animosity between her and the rest of my family. Almost daily I would hear how bad my family was treating her, talking about her, or spreading rumors about her. She was very sensitive and very defensive about everything. She had a difficult time getting along with just about anyone in the family. This ultimately made me decide to stay away from my brothers and sisters altogether.

I did it because I was caught in the middle of trying to keep the peace between them all. Even though it was not the right thing for me to do, I just wanted your mother to be happy. She showed jealousy towards anyone who came close to me, whether it was family or friends. So I decided to give her the benefit of the doubt by spending more time together to see if, in fact, it was my family who was the cause of her attitude or if it was something else.

Inside myself, I was hurt because I love a close family, but my wife was more important, and so it was that we started to just focus on our own family, and, at times, I would not see a brother or a sister for weeks, even though we lived five minutes away from each other.

While your mother was in constant contact with her parents and brothers, she was not easily adjusting to her new life in America. She was homesick for quite a long time. And as much as I tried to boost her confidence level, she was still not the happy and outgoing person I had for so long hoped to find. Month in, month out, I was dealing with this, and before you knew it, I was slowly distancing myself from your mother. She was extremely difficult to communicate with, even on the smallest of subjects.

Stubbornness can devastate a relationship. It became increasingly difficult to reason with your mother. She had never worked outside the home, which was fine with me. I never made her do anything she didn't want to do. I suggested that she find a job or even volunteer for free, just to get out of the house and feel like she was doing something for herself, but she would not do it. I suggested that I open a business for her to stay busy, but she chose not to do that either. I just wanted her to have some confidence and feel good about herself, but I would get the same stubborn answers. It seemed that I could not do anything to make her happy.

I was trying very hard to get our marriage on the right track and tried to resolve our differences with the family so that we could all get along. Forgiveness was so difficult for your mother. She could not move past the hatred and resentment she had come to harbor in her heart for my family during the short time she had known everyone. I, personally, forgive very easily and your mother hated that about me. She found so many wrongs in people and did not easily trust anyone. After a while we found ourselves without many friends or relatives or family we could be close to. She wanted me on her side, and by her side, at all times.

Life became difficult to deal with at home. She was not content with anything we had: the house we lived in, the cars we drove, the job I had, or our friends and family. She wanted us to move to another city away from everybody. Of course, my answer was, "No, because no matter where we moved to," I told her; "unless you change yourself and the way you deal with problems, you are never going to be happy, even if we moved to the moon." But she would not be convinced of that. And so we continued to live our life pretending to have a normal marriage.

It had been a tough year so far as we celebrated our first year anniversary. We wanted things to be better, and things would take a turn the day she had morning sickness. She called me at work and informed me that she was not feeling well. She described her feelings to me and, instantly, I had a feeling of incredible joy in my heart. I told her that she may be pregnant with our baby boy. I was joking with her and couldn't wait to get home with a pregnancy test I would stop to buy on my way. She was very nervous, as was I. But I was more excited about it.

When I got home and gave her the pregnancy test, she went into the bathroom, but came out a few minutes later with what seemed like disappointment. I asked, "Well are we having a boy?" She was silent. I took the test from her and found it to be positive. I jumped with excitement and hugged her and kissed her.

We called a doctor and made an appointment to check the validity of the pregnancy test. We were officially told that we were having a baby, and your mother was about a month along. The doctor instructed us on what to do and what to expect, and we went home.

My life was finally on track, I thought. It was very exciting now being married and starting a family. Every day I would call her from work to check up on her and see if she was doing well. She was scared and I wanted to make sure she knew that she was not alone in this. But her attitude was not encouraging.

She went into a little depression and was not herself anymore. I couldn't help but wonder what, if anything, was going to make this girl happy if not our first born? I made sure that she was not being bothered by anyone in the family, by staying away from them. I made sure that she had a new car so not to always depend on me. She had credit cards and plenty of cash in the safe. I was spoiling her with flowers and gifts and, most importantly, support for what she was going through.

Two months passed and still she was not as happy as I would like to have seen her. So I began to talk about that to my friends and sought their advice. I was told that it was normal for women to feel that way during the first pregnancy and that I should not worry. This would all change the day I came home from work and found your mother upstairs in a very disturbing state of mind.

I asked if she was okay but got no response, as she was busy looking at a computer screen. I walked over and asked her what she was doing and, to my horror, she said that she was researching online and had found a doctor that could perform an abortion on her, and she added that she did not need my permission to do it.

My heart dropped and my jaw froze. I could not believe what I was hearing. I remember that my hands were shaking and my knees wanted to give out. It felt like I was in a horror movie, and I had to take a breath and evaluate the situation for a minute. *Is this for real or did I just misunderstand,* I thought. I went to my knees and held her in my arms and cried. "Are you okay?" I asked. "Did you take any medicine? Do you feel sick?"

Of all the things one can prepare for, this is not one of them. I did not know how to react. Part of me was in shock, and the other was trying to rationalize with her. I began to console her and tell her that what she was going through was normal and that many women go through this. "You are just scared," I said, "and you are young and it's your first pregnancy. Don't worry. I'm right here with you. We are going to be okay."

While I was speaking, my mind drifted, replaying what I might have said or done to possibly cause this. I began to blame myself for making her feel this way, but I could come up with nothing. I then blamed myself for rushing into a marriage to someone I hardly knew anything about. *Is it possible that she had some mental issues in her past that no one told me about?* I asked myself.

For the next few hours, we continued to talk so that I could get an idea of where this craziness was coming from. I asked her if someone had been talking with her about abortions or was it all her own thinking. She was so calm and so matter-of-fact about getting an abortion that I was scared to even raise my voice with the anger that I had. I kept calm and just listened to the sickening words that kept coming out of her mouth.

She said that she was too young to be tied down with a baby and that we could always have another one at a later date. She continued by saying that it was her body and she was going to make the decision of what was good for her and that, while she was new in this country, she knew her rights to make such decisions.

I began to ask her a few questions to get a better understanding of her mental state. "Do you love me?" I asked.

"Yes," she answered.

I took her back to the time I had asked her to marry me and reminded her that we both had an understanding that we would live in America. "Is that not right?" I asked. "And you knew that you were going to leave your family and start your new life with me away from them, right? This is what married people do, they start a family, and a part of starting a family is the responsibility of having children.

"It is not just one person here who makes these decisions," I continued. "I also am the father and have equal obligations and responsibilities towards our child. You are just stressing out and maybe just nervous or overwhelmed with things, but I'm here with you. You are not alone, we will make it and we will have a beautiful child and you will see that it will be worth all the pain. Just trust me and in a few days you will feel good and all of this will be behind us."

It was an exhausting day and mentally draining. I'm not sure what she was thinking as we both tried to get some sleep. But I, personally, was scared of what she might do while I went to work the next day. The thought of her meeting a non-licensed doctor in some dark alley kept making its way into my head, and I had no idea how to deal with this. I did not want anyone in the family to know what I was going through, as it would almost be the one thing they needed to hear to confirm what they have been saying about your mother all along. So this was something I would have to handle on my own.

Your mother was a smart girl and was more mature than the typical twenty-two-year-old girls I have met. She was known to be a good writer and some of her writings and poetry were even published in some small newspapers while she was in Syria. She had read a lot of books, and for someone who had only been in the country a little over a year, she spoke and understood the English language like someone who had been here for years. She would watch television while I was at work and then share with me the day's events on talk shows like Oprah or Dr. Phil.

The following couple of weeks would be the most difficult, as I would go to work with my heart and my mind filled with mixed emotions and fear. On one hand I was always worried about your mother's state of mind and what she might be capable of doing while I was away. And on the other, I was trying to be supportive and encouraging. I was extra cautious about what I would say, to the point where I had to think about the sentence before it rolled off of my tongue, for the fear of upsetting her in any way. All of this just so we could get through what felt like a nightmare and not jeopardize the health of our child.

Sometimes I would call friends or relatives to stop by our house and have some coffee with your mother while I was at work. I thought she might open up to one of them, and perhaps she would get some advice that was not coming from me personally.

Of course she never knew that I did that. Up until that point, she did not want anyone to know that we are even having a child. She had asked me not to share the news with my family. Of course this was very difficult for any man to do. I did share the news with my friends only, not family. Meanwhile, I was doing my best to show her how much I loved her and how our life was going to be after we had our first baby. I would take her shopping and look at all the wonderful children's clothing and nursery themes. We would stay up at night and try to come up with names for boys and some for girls and she began to show some interest. Perhaps this whole thing was just a freak moment of insanity and soon it would all be over.

Every month we would go and visit with her doctor and soon we were able to hear the baby's heartbeat and some movement. She finally woke up from the nightmare of wanting an abortion.

From then on she was more accepting of her role as an expecting mother. This is not to say I was completely at ease, but at least she was not talking of abortions any more. She had grown fond of my mother and father and would visit with them more often. She said that they were the only ones who understood her and always supported her.

One day, while I was at work, I received a call from your mother that she was lying on the floor and could not move. She said that she had been trying to lift something heavy and pulled her back and fell to the floor. I dropped everything at work and drove home, as it was only ten minutes away. On the way there I was concerned about your mother but more so about our unborn child. You mother had now been pregnant for about four months with our baby. When I arrived at the house, she was on the sofa and was unable to move without some pain. I knew a little about what she was feeling, as I, too, had pulled a muscle before and had gone through similar pain. However, she was with child and I did not want to take any chances.

I took her straight to the urgent care and explained to them what had happened. They prescribed some light medicine and sports cream and advised her to get some rest and to stay away from lifting any heavy items, as it was not healthy for our child.

A couple of days later we had an appointment with her doctor for a routine monthly checkup. The doctor was a wonderful person from Persia. She showed us images of our baby and had us hear the heartbeat again. She said that we had a very healthy and normal baby. I liked this part when the doctor was showing us where certain parts of our baby were and how it was curled up. She asked if we wanted to know what sex the baby was; we both had agreed that we wanted to know. She said. "You are having a baby boy." I was elated and a relief came over me. I sighed and was smiling all the way to your grandparent's house, where we decided to share the news of my baby boy.

For the next few days, we would focus on redecorating one of the rooms and start shopping for our baby boy. On the days that I was off, I was painting the baby's room and things were getting better between us. I came home one day and your mother was lying on the couch in pain. I asked what the matter was and she said that she had taken a fall on the stairs while carrying a load of laundry. I was furious for a moment, as I had told her over and over not to do anything strenuous as it may hurt our child. She was upset and said, "All you care about is your child. You don't care about me."

I assured her that that was not the case. "I care about both of you," I said. "But you need to be careful at this stage of your pregnancy. Remember what the doctor told you?"

The next day she was still in pain. So I called a chiropractor to see if maybe a back adjustment might help alleviate some of the pain. We informed the doctor that she was pregnant, which meant that he needed to be extra cautious. After a few moments she was back home, and a few days later she was back to herself again. She did not like the morning sickness and I suggested she call her doctor to prescribe some medicine for that. She reminded me that we had an appointment in a few days, anyway, and that she would ask the doctor at that time.

I had the day off on the day of your mother's routine doctor's visit and decided to tag along with her. This time we wanted to collect a video of the baby's movement, which I said was a good idea. The doctor had your mother lay down as she prepared the video equipment and the ultrasound wand.

She asked your mother how she had been feeling and if there was anything she was concerned about. Your mother told her that she was having bad morning sickness and asked if she would recommend some medicine. The doctor assured her that she would. The doctor began to move the ultrasound wand over the belly, time and time again. She was having a hard time hearing a heartbeat. So she went back and checked her equipment. After a minor adjustment she tried again, but this time she stopped and asked to be excused for a moment to bring another machine. As she left, I was not comfortable with the way she was acting.

I began to think the worst. I'm not sure why I felt that way; I really did not have a good reason. But, nonetheless, I began to pray in my head for everything to be okay. Moments later the doctor came back, this time with an assistant. They seemed pretty calm, so I removed the bad thoughts from my head and waited as they ran more tests. After they were done testing, the doctor simply asked your mother to sit up and then the assistant walked us over to an office close by. "The doctor will be with you in a moment to talk with you," she said.

"Is everything okay?" I asked.

"Yes," she said, "but the doctor will discuss the details with you." Then she just walked out.

Your mother and I were very quiet, not saying much. The doctor walked in and sat at her desk across from us, looked us in the face, and said, "I'm so sorry to tell you this, but your baby is not showing any signs of a heartbeat after numerous tests."

It was the worst news anyone can hear. We both began to cry as the doctor continued talking to us about what the next steps were. I began to question the doctor about what might have caused this, as the baby was showing healthy on every visit. She just gave me one scenario after another, and one statistic after another, and how many parents go through this. She said that it was not our fault, and that things like this can happen for a number of reasons. She continued saying that we might find the reason after they delivered the baby.

My body was numb and my mind was a blur. I wanted an answer that could satisfy me. I hugged your mother as she cried; I tried to comfort her and be the strong one here, but I needed comfort myself. I was devastated. I told the doctor that there were no signs that anything was wrong. "How could this happen," I asked. "Is it possible that the machine is wrong?"

She just shook her head and again said, "I'm sorry."

I'm not sure what happened the few days after that. All I can remember is a big disconnect between me and your mother, me and God, and me and the world. I felt empty and sick to my stomach. The one thing I've wanted ever since I was a young man was to have a baby I could call my own and now God took it away from me. I gave your mother as much support as I could. I took a few days off from work to be with her, as we tried to console one another and tried to figure out how we could deal with this tragedy.

After talking with many people and friends, they all seemed to say the same things. Some would say, "God knows what He is doing" and that we should have some faith that it happened for a reason. Others would tell us that they, too, went through it and that it was normal. But I, personally, did not think that there was anything normal about it. However, God helped us through it and, day after day, it became easier and easier. I never blamed your mother even once nor did I display any negative attitude towards her. But, deep in my heart, I was not at all happy.

Every day I would replay incidents and episodes your mother and I had had regarding her intention to have an abortion, and I couldn't help but wonder if all of that had anything to do with us losing our baby boy. The anger I harbored in my heart would, at times, cause me to think of walking away from your mother. I thought that maybe this was a sign from God that we did not belong together. After all, it had not been a happy marriage from the beginning, and since now we did not have any children to worry about, I thought ending the marriage would be best for both of us.

My conscience was full of guilt for even thinking of leaving your mother at this point, and I thought that I was being selfish. I decided that I would stay and make this marriage work. As time passed, we began to get along more and became closer. It seemed that your mother had matured more in the last few months and was beginning to show more interest in my family again.

A year or so later we were pregnant again, and this time we had a most beautiful baby girl who would change our lives forever. That baby girl was you! You were so beautiful and slowly became the answer to our prayers. We were now a family and you were the center of it all. We finally could smile wholeheartedly and start doing family activities and birthday parties.

Chapter 2

During the next two years, our family would suffer the loss of my mother and, a few months later, the loss of my father. This would be devastating for our whole family as, for the first time in the history of our family, all six sisters and four brothers were finally together in America. My parents' home was the one place where we all gathered and felt safe and comfortable. Now we would all disperse in different directions.

Three years later after you were born, to the day, we were once again blessed with another beautiful and healthy baby girl. I couldn't have been happier. We were financially in good shape, I had a healthy family and, for the most part, things were good between your mother and me. I was very happy with your mom when she gave birth to your little sister, and I gave her a very expensive diamond cross as a gift, just like I gave her a very expensive diamond ring when you were born. I wanted her to feel good and also show her how much I loved her and appreciated her raising our two girls.

In 2008 your grandparents on your mother's side came to America to visit us from Syria. Your mother had become a U.S. citizen around that time. I thought that our marriage was going well, but she was moving further away from me. I would spend the next two years dealing with her depression, mood swings and stubbornness. She started to act differently and would not participate in our everyday things. Things like going to the park. I would take you both to the park without her. I would say, 'Let's all go fishing,' but she would say, 'Take the girls and go, I want to stay home.'

I would take you and your sister to the arcade or to the lake or anywhere and still she would not go with us. We would eat breakfast together, but she would not join us. I would cook dinner and she would choose to be in her room. We found ourselves being disconnected, and I just could not understand her or her actions. Over time it made us fall out of love with each other. We both loved our girls in our own way and that was the only thing that was keeping us together.

On January 12th I decided to baptize you and your sister and take advantage of your grandparents being in America. I planned a most beautiful party for all of us to enjoy. Over three hundred people came to celebrate with us. And the party went very well. Your mother's brother was given the honor of being your godfather, against my wishes, but I had to do it to please your mother. And one of my dear friends was given the honor of being your sister's godfather. This friend was a good man and very religious. That was one of the proudest moments for me, seeing both of you baptized.

Later that same year, the world economy experienced the most challenging times in fifty years. The housing market crashed, the financial market was a disaster, banks were going bankrupt, and the stock market crashed. People lost their fortunes, homes and jobs. Things were looking very bad for most people.

Thank God our family did not suffer much, and even though I was making half the money I used to make, I never let your mother feel that there was anything wrong. We continued to spend the same amount of money and our lifestyle did not change; we were very blessed and, thank God, we went through the bad times with minor losses.

We celebrated Christmas Eve 2009 and the next day we all woke up to open the presents. And like usual, it was very exciting, and everyone was happy. Not long after that your mother and I started to grow more distant, and I was at that point where I needed to do something. I tried to ask your mother numerous times what was wrong, but she would not say. I was worried that I was slowly losing my marriage and began to ask other people for advice.

Some said that we needed some time away from each other. Some said that we needed to go to a counselor and others said we needed to talk to a priest. Your mother was not talking to me much and we just tried to make it day by day.

At work I was not myself and it was evident to one of my dear friends there. We spent most of the day together. We were both finance managers and had similar backgrounds. He was from Afghanistan and I, of course, was from Syria. He was a trusted friend and I shared with him many of the things that were taking place in my marriage. He shared with me some of the things in his marriage and tried to console me and make me feel better.

He would always say that most marriages go through what I was going through, and I should just be patient and try to work it out. But one night, while I was at work and could not focus on anything, a thought crossed my mind that I didn't want to entertain even for a moment. Was my wife possibly being unfaithful and seeing another man? Was it possible that was the reason she had been so distant all this time?

My mind began to take me back and replay certain days and certain occasions when she would act really strange. Was it possible? My heart was pounding really hard. I got this sick feeling in my stomach, but I needed to be sure. I decided to go online and pull a copy of the most recent phone bill to see if I could detect any strange numbers on it. Part of me did not want to know, but I could not stop my curiosity. This is what married people fear more than anything. An unfaithful spouse. I logged on, dreading to see the results. I printed the summery of the last month and, as I began to scroll down the pages, I noticed a number that was not only unfamiliar to me, but practically occupied the whole page.

On January 25, 2010, your mother and I had a big fight and things got worse as she told me that she no longer wanted to be with me and that she no longer had any feelings of love for me. I was devastated to find that, in her own words, she had not had any feelings for me for the last two years. This would shed some light on why things had been that way between us for so long. I was very disappointed with her and hurt. It's hard to explain what I was going through, because part of me was angry, while another part was rejoicing in the fact that I could finally move on with my life and be away from this miserable person.

I was now faced with the reality of dissolving our marriage of eight years. Of course the first thing I thought of was you and your sister. It is one thing to be faced with a divorce, that part was easy to swallow. After all, a relationship that lacks trust is nothing short of a disaster waiting to happen. Without trust you may as well be walking a tight rope without a net. But I could not bear to think about the idea of you and your sister having to deal with the psychological effects of a split family. I knew I was in a tough predicament and I needed to find a way to fix it.

One day I suggested going to counseling to deal with this very embarrassing situation. Your mother reluctantly agreed. I wanted our marriage to work and I did not want to end up in a divorce, even though that was the first thing that crossed my mind when I ultimately confronted her about the phone bill. She gave me a story of how it was nothing at all like it seemed. She said that the reason she was talking to another man was that she was not getting any emotional support from me, and she had found someone who listened to her and understood what she was going through. She swore on your life that nothing had happened between them other than conversations. Whether I truly believed her or not is irrelevant, and, after much soul searching, I forgave her, and we started to go to counseling once a week. But after three visits I was still not seeing any improvements or even any interest or willingness from your mother to work things out.

Traditionally, when there are marital issues, I have always heard from others that a church pastor can usually be an option to resolve differences between couples. So I decided to invite our church pastor, who your mother respected, to talk to us, and she agreed. He came over to our house and we shared our problems with him. It was a drawn out evening, and, while there was a lot of mudslinging and much blame and finger-pointing, I was pleased with the outcome. Your mom, on the other hand, once again took everything personally and she became more distant from me and the family.

I felt, at this point, that staying in the marriage just for the sake of my children was not healthy for anyone. I needed to make a decision and soon. It sounds easy in theory to just walk away and everyone just go their separate ways. But I was still not a hundred percent convinced that we couldn't somehow manage to resolve our issues. *There must be something else we can try to save this marriage,* I thought.

A few days later your mother asked me if she could go to visit her brother in northern California and spend Easter there. At first I did not like the idea of being away from my family on Easter, but then I thought that maybe this is what we needed but had not yet tried. *A little time away from one another may be what is missing,* I decided. I drove you all to the airport and expected you back in ten days.

While your mother visited with her brother, I had time to reflect on my life and seek advice from family and friends. They convinced me to put my pride aside and think about the positive things about your mother and the good qualities she had and really put forth an effort to make our marriage work. I sent your mom an email telling her how much I loved her and how I wanted things to work out between us. I told her how much I appreciated her and the way she raised our girls, that I forgave her for what she had done to me, and that I was hopeful that she would read the email and call me to say the same thing.

Her response was heartless. She sent me a message saying, "Your words are eight years too late." She said that she did not feel the same about me. I was once again very hurt and disappointed.

I picked the three of you up at the airport around the 25th of April, 2010, and when we got home, things were very dry between your mother and me. She seemed very confused and preoccupied with things in her mind, but she would not share them with me. I knew that the situation was now at its most serious and I really wanted your mother to give me a final answer about her feelings towards me and the future of our marriage. We had a chance to discuss the email that I had sent her and I shared with her how hurt I was to receive her response.

We decided for the first time to have a constructive dialogue one evening and made an agreement that there would not be any yelling or disrespect or finger-pointing. We agreed to be honest, civil, and mature. "Let's put it all on the table and try to come up with the best way to resolve our differences," I said. "If we come to terms, great. But, if we cannot, then we are going to do everything in our power to make it as civil as possible to ensure that our children do not pay the price for our mistakes."

It was so refreshing to see your mother like that. Perhaps the time apart was a good idea after all. She began to tell me how we needed to really put an effort into resolving our issues. And that, if I really wanted this marriage to work, and I really meant what I had said in the email, she would also try and make our marriage work. We each decided to really open up and share our true feelings and what bothered us about each other. We were to be honest, without fear of retaliation or outbursts from the other person.

I asked her to start. She went on to tell me about how she felt neglected emotionally and how she needed me to be more supportive of her dreams and ambitions. She recalled the times when she felt unloved and unworthy. She needed me to be more open and to share with her my feelings.

I listened and acknowledged everything she said. And I also began to tell her about the things that I liked about her and the things that drove me away.

"Let's agree to be more conscious of each other's feelings and avoid the things that drive us apart or cause tension," I told her.

We both felt a sense of relief and, for once in a long time, we walked away from the conversation with semi-positive attitudes.

Chapter 3

Little did I know what was going on in her mind. I was under the impression that we were trying to work things out. Not long after she got back from her brother's, her attitude and demeanor were unusual. She was a little more carefree. And while we were not back to a normal relationship, things were getting more bearable.

A few days later she asked me if she could take you and your sister to Syria to visit her ailing parents, who wanted to see their grandchildren, and to also take some time to think about our marriage and our recent conversation about working things out. I was encouraged to hear that but totally against the idea of her going to Syria. I suggested that she call her parents and invite them to come visit us here in America. She added that she really missed her sister and relatives there, as well.

Every day that passed she would try to convince me that going to Syria would somehow fix our issues. And the more I resisted the idea, the more distant and withdrawn she became. You would ask me, 'Why is mommy sleeping down stairs, and 'Why is mommy not eating with us? Why is mommy not going anywhere with us?' It was breaking my heart that I couldn't tell you.

After your mother asked me almost every day to go to Syria and being very persistent, I finally agreed. I was not happy with my decision, especially that she wanted to go to Syria a few days prior to your 6th birthday and your sister's 3rd birthday. "Why don't you wait 'til we celebrate the girls' birthdays and then you can go," I said. But she insisted that we would celebrate your birthdays a few days before.

I bought the tickets and she started planning what to take with her. And before long there were over six bags full of things. When I asked why she needed so many things when she was only going to be in Syria for two months, she got upset and said it was her business. I thought nothing of it.

About a week before the flight date, your mother was acting differently, but I could not tell what it was. She had gone to Syria with you before, but this time she was not acting normal at all. And as for my family, I had not shared any of the marital problems with anyone, not even my close brother. After all, everyone thought that we had the perfect marriage.

The time was here and on June 28, 2010, I drove you, your sister and mother to the airport. The trip was to be a little over two months and then you were to be back on September 6, just in time to go back to school on the 7th. I was not myself that day and all the way to the airport your mother and I did not speak much.

I had an uneasy feeling in my stomach. I was upset with your mom that she was taking you away from me, but I thought it would be a sacrifice to save our marriage. At the airport, your mom was very nervous and she would not sit down. She would not even make eye contact with me. I was not at all at ease. I asked if we could go upstairs and have a bite to eat before your flight, and that made her even more nervous. Even though it was not the time or the place to start a conversation about any serious issues, I felt the need to ask if there was something we needed to talk about, but she said, "No, we will talk when we get back."

We did not finish our food, as she was pacing back and forth. I thought to myself, *my goodness, does she want to leave that bad?* I said, "Let's go," and I walked with you to the line where passengers only can cross. There I gathered you and you sister and asked you to be good girls and to not to give your mother a hard time. I assured you that time would fly by and before you knew it, you would be back and that I would miss you. You began to move in line and waving 'bye to me. You were both blowing me kisses as the tears went down my face behind my sunglasses. I did not want you to see your dad crying. Your mother had a different look, however; she looked at me with dead eyes that showed no expression, like she was getting away with something. And I did not like that look.

A second later you disappeared and I could see you no more and my heart fell to the ground. I could not stop crying and something in my heart was telling me that something was wrong, but I did not know what to do. I just drove home, crying the whole way, and praying that you would get there safely. *Go back and stop the airplane*, my mind would tell me. But I continued driving to a lifeless, empty house.

June 30, 2010, you arrived in Syria and I got a chance to talk to you and your mom to make sure that you had arrived safely. Thank God, everything went well. I did notice something in your mother's voice right away. She sounded like she was being bothered by my phone call and I was upset about that, but I dismissed it. I thought it must be jet lag. I just said, *"Al hamd lilla 3al salami"* (Thank God you made it safely). I talked briefly with you and your sister and we hung up. I called every day for the first week, and then it was every other day for the following week. But every time I would speak with your mother, our conversation would be short and dry. I figured that she needed to spend time with her family and I did not want to put any pressure on her or discuss our marriage issues.

I called your mother after you had been in Syria about two weeks and asked if she had had some time to think about us and our marriage. She said she had but that she needed more time. I told her that I had missed her and our girls and said that maybe it would be best if she would cut her vacation by a couple weeks so that I, too, could spend time with you before you went back to school. She said, "Since we are here already, and since it's been a long time since I have seen my family, it would be better to stay for the duration."

At this point I was working a lot, and I would come home exhausted. But I missed you so much, I would spend most of the night watching old home movies of you and your sister and the many trips we had taken. The more I watched, the more I wanted you back home as soon as possible.

Since the time difference between us was now about twelve hours, I would call you after midnight to say good morning. One evening while I was watching some movies, I called and talked with your mother and expressed to her that I could no longer focus on my work or anything else and that I really wanted her to pack her bags and come back home as soon as possible. I told her that I missed my girls and I wanted her to call the travel agent and get the next flight out. Her response would bring me to my knees. She said that not only was she not coming back soon but that she was *never* coming back.

She seemed more relaxed this time, a little more confident. She went on to unload an arsenal of accusations towards me that went back to our wedding day and all the way to the present. I could not get a word in. It was an incredible display of drama like you've never heard, not even in the movies. It sounded like she had written these things down like a script.

First, it started slow with statements that I was never supportive of her or her dreams. Then she claimed that I was not paying attention to her and that I did not protect her from my family, as though my family was some gang or a militant group.

I tried to respond to these concerns in a diplomatic and rational way, only because I knew I was helpless from thousands of miles away. Without overreacting, I just listened and took all the verbal abuse and disrespect and blame and lies from her because, in the back of my mind, I thought she was going crazy or that she was on some bad medication. And worse than that, she had my children in another country.

So I did all I could to calm her down and try to reason with her, but she would not cooperate or listen to anything I had to say. *This is just a bad dream,* I thought. *Has she gone absolutely mad?* I felt helpless. On one hand, I had to be nice and calm in order to get to the bottom of what she was thinking and, on the other hand, I needed to think of you and your sister and how I could make her just bring you back safely. I was not prepared for what was to come.

The following day, and after thinking about things at home by myself, I realized that the situation with your mother was now very serious. I called to talk with you and this time I started to hear a different voice from your mother; she was more heartless than the day before. And as much as I tried to talk with her to resolve our issues, the more issues she raised. She started telling her family about our situation and, before you knew it, everyone knew that we were fighting. She repeated what she had said before, that she would not be coming back to America, not now or ever, and that Syria was now her home and she was keeping you and your sister. She added that if I wanted to see you and your sister, it was going to be on her terms and on her turf.

What the hell is she talking about? What is going on here? This is crazy. I felt like I was now talking to some kidnapper who was making demands. I lost my temper and I was not able to keep my nice composure at this point. I began to really talk to her like she had truly lost her mind. The first thing I said was, "Listen to what you are saying. This is insane. Whatever problems we have, we can resolve them here in America. Our girls don't have to pay the price for our mistakes. This is not the way to deal with our problems; we live here in America, our children go to school here, and we need to resolve our differences here. Now, please, I beg you, just take a few days and say good-bye to your family, and please come back with our girls before school starts." Nothing I said made a single dent. She had made up her mind and now I needed to deal with it.

Needless to say, I did not sleep a minute that night. A million thoughts went through my mind; none were nice or rational. I blamed myself for agreeing to this trip and the guilt was overwhelming. *How can I be so stupid and blind? How did I get talked into this?*

I called the next day with the hopes that it was just a bad dream. She answered the phone.

"Listen," I said, "I don't want to fight or argue, let's just talk rationally."

"There is nothing to talk about," she said. "Here is what you can do. You can come and visit with our girls once a year and go back to America. I do not want to go back to America any more. This is my home now in Syria, this is where I was born and here is where I will live, like it or not. I hate America and everyone in it."

I just lost my mind when I heard that. You can only imagine what that might feel like. I was now panicking and worrying about what you and your sister were going through. I did not know if this was my wife I was talking to or some crazy person. She started to tell her family a bunch of exaggerations and lies, which until now I had not thought that she would do. Blatant lie after lie, and I was not there to defend myself or clarify to them that what she was saying was not true. Initially, she started to tell them that I was not romantic enough, and I did not speak romantic words to her, and that I was too dry with her.

After dismissing that nonsense, her family would talk to me and they would laugh at how silly our issues were. They said that in comparison to other people's problems, we were in heaven. And they were right. We did have a life that most people dreamed of. So when she saw that she was not getting much sympathy from her family, she started to tell them that the stress that she was going through was causing her to have high blood pressure and other health problems. She began to take some medicine when she got to Syria. Funny, for the nine years that we were together, and the thousands of dollars of health insurance that we had paid for, she did not once tell me nor did she ever mention that she had a health problem. But now, all of the sudden, she was a sick and helpless victim. Her family started to side with her and now they were all against me.

Chapter 4

A month or so had passed since she took you to that dreaded place. When I'd call to talk to you and your sister, I'd go through hell trying to get someone to pick up the phone. I would call over twenty times before one of them would pick up the phone one time. I was getting more worried. I couldn't help but think the worst. The helpless feeling of not knowing where you were and where you were going killed me. Your mom's family was being very vague about your whereabouts. They would make up reasons why I was not able to talk to you, time and again.

I decided to get other people involved. Prominent people and family members who I thought might change your mother's mind. Traditionally, every family had an elder who would act as the mediator and advisor when the need arose. Your mother's family had looked up to the grandfather. I called to talk with him and shared with him my concern about your mother and what she was doing. He seemed to side with me. But when he called to set up a visit with your mother and the rest of the family, he was turned away and was told not to interfere. This was embarrassing to a man who was trying to be a peacemaker. It proved that they were not only inconsiderate but very disrespectful.

Meanwhile your mother was working behind the scene, trying to make you and your sister official Syrian citizens so that she could make sure you could not leave the country. She had to forge many documents, due to the fact that, normally, the father would have to be present.

The next time I spoke with your mother, she informed me that she had studied the laws in Syria and that I would have no rights there if I were to try getting you back to America. She had been planning this for a long time before she went to Syria. She knew that the law was on her side. I, on the other hand, did not know anything. I just thought, *my girls are American citizens and all I have to do is call the U.S. Embassy and they will have them back in twenty-four hours.* That would prove far from reality.

By now I had exhausted all peaceful avenues. I listened to young and old, friend and foe, and now I needed to make a decision. I spoke with your mother to get her final answer. She said that she had made up her mind to stay in Syria and that there was nothing else to talk about. At this point there was only about ten days before your vacation was to be over. I was devastated to hear that news. She was very cold and disrespectful towards me and my feelings. It seemed to me that she was using you and your sister as tools to achieve her objective.

"The laws in Syria are different," she warned me. "You don't have the rights here like you do in America. Syria is my home turf," she went on. You should watch your back."

She was almost waging a war. She was losing her mind and her sense of humanity. It was as though she never knew me.

I called her brother in America a couple of days before your vacation was to be over and insisted he talk to his sister and convince her to come back and bring my girls back. I assured him that if she came back, I would give her all that I owned, from money to home to cars, and also pay for her monthly expenses and, even If she wanted a divorce, I would give her that, just bring my girls back.

After over an hour of trying to make sense to him, he reiterated that she would not be coming back. I always knew that he had no influence or a backbone, but I wanted to exhaust every option.

I explained to him that I had no choice but to go to court and proceed legally. He took what I said to be a threat to him and your mother. I went on to tell him that for the last two months I had tried to do everything the civil way, the family and traditional way, the godly way and still they had rejected every idea. Now I must fight for my girls any which way I could, and If they did not show up at the scheduled time to America, which was a couple days later, I would assume that she had abducted my girls and that now we would let the justice system work.

Monday, September 7, 2010, would come and go like any other day. I had been waiting for this day for two months and now it would mean absolutely nothing because your mother had decided to stay in Syria for good.

I was heartbroken and my mind was filled with hatred and resentment towards your mother and her criminal family. Needless to say, I had some unpleasant thoughts towards them as I tried to contemplate my options. *They have taken my baby girls away from me. They have tricked me and are now using my daughters as bargaining chips. If only I was there . . . I'm not sure what I would do. But no time for that now, I need to come up with a way to get my girls back.*

Thus far, I was not sharing any of my feelings with anyone except one of my closest friends. I was trying to hide the things your mom was doing so as to not embarrass her or our family. Of course my family was concerned, and when your mother did not show up as scheduled, all hell broke loose. I was bombarded with phone calls from my sisters and brothers asking if everything was okay and why your mother had not come back. I simply said that she was not feeling well enough to travel and had decided to extend her stay for a little while longer. That triggered a barrage of curiosity, and before long, rumors began to spring up in certain circles in the community.

I was having dinner at my older brother's house one night and the discussion was entirely about your mother. I was shocked to learn that your mother had been discussing our marital affairs with my brother and his wife. I was confronted by many questions that, up until that point, I thought were private between your mother and me. I guess I was so blind. They asked me about the counseling that your mother and I had attended. It was embarrassing to me, but I wanted to know how much your mother had shared with them.

They began to tell me some of the things that your mother had been sharing with them for the last couple of months prior to her leaving for Syria. She had told them that I was a difficult man to deal with and that I was treating her so badly. She was crying to them about how unhappy she was with our relationship at home. When I asked them why they had not shared this information with me, they said that she begged them not to tell me or to interfere.

They went on to tell me that she had mentioned going to Syria and they encouraged her to do so. If only I had known that, I may have exercised a different decision to let her leave with you and your sister.

Now I had to figure out what my legal rights were here in America and there in Syria. I started to ask people some questions about Syrian law and spent many hours researching it online. I was very disappointed to find that, due to the fact that you and your sister had Syrian parents, it meant that you were automatically considered Syrian citizens. And being Syrian citizens meant that you were protected under their civil and legal code.

I began my quest to get you and your sister back by calling the FBI. They are responsible for investigating missing and abducted children. This step was pretty difficult for me to do. Taking you was a serious offense, and I had tried to resolve it with your mother privately, but I was not getting a single sign from her or anyone else that you might come back home. My hands were tied and, at that point, I did not feel that I had any other choice than to bring in official help.

I shared my story with the FBI, hoping that they would spring into action, assemble a team, and have you back in my arms in a matter of days. However, they offered no assistance and said, "There is nothing we can do at this juncture." They said I needed to call the State Department in Washington to see what they would advise. I called the State Department and after three days a lady named Ann McGahuey called me back.

"I'm sorry. There is nothing I can do to help, even though your children are American citizens," she told me when I explained my story to her. Then she went on to inform me that Syria does not abide by the Hague convention treaty that nations had signed to protect children from this sort of thing and that I needed to go to a local court and have a judge issue an order in writing so that an agency could take action to help me.

I was very frustrated by this news because I always thought that, being a U.S. citizen, I was more protected than that. We talked about Interpol and how they might assist in retrieving you should your mother travel to another country that does recognize international law. Ms. McGahuey said that if I could somehow talk your mother into meeting with me in France, for instance, she would have Interpol stop her and force her to come back to America. This, of course, after I had a valid court order.

I began to research information on the justice system and found that a lawyer would be necessary here and in Syria. I looked for a good lawyer and made an appointment to see him to discuss my options in America.

I instructed my lawyer to help me with filing a court order to send to your mother so that she would be forced to bring you and your sister back. After filing, we were given a court date set for the 20th of September. I felt good about my progress so far. I felt as though I was doing everything in my power at that point.

I was still trying to resolve the issue with your mother on the phone. I was not able to pinpoint a specific reason why anyone would want to leave a home in America for another home in Syria. People from around the world do anything to come here. I couldn't help but wonder if there was an old love who she might be interested in. Why else would someone do this? She had always spoken of old friends from school, but I did not have proof. It would actually have been less painful if she would have just told me that. I might have understood. I cannot believe that she didn't understand how difficult it was for me to be away from my girls; to her it was no big deal, since she was with you and your sister, while I could not sleep for months.

Up until this point, I really thought that a court order would do the trick and, once issued, it would scare your mother and make her come back. As for me going to Syria to try to resolve our issues, that was not an easy option. I had to ask permission from the Syrian Embassy in Washington, D.C. to be able to travel to Syria.

There are always risks involved in traveling to Syria for me. For men who are born in Syria, it is mandatory for them to serve in the military. And since I had left the country prior to being of age, it meant that I still had an obligation to serve should I go back. Unless I obtained an exception from the Syrian authorities to visit at a specific time that is set by their president. I called and had them send me an application. I would have to wait and wait. One month passed and then two months, and still I did not get an approval. I was calling the Syrian Embassy almost daily trying to see why they had not sent me the approval and I would get the same answer every time. "Just wait."

I was still having a hard time calling you. After many attempts, I finally got a chance to talk with your mother. I explained to her that what she was doing was not only illegal but was going to have long term effects on your future and your sister's. I told her that she needed to come back to America and resolve our issues the right way so that both of you could grow up with a father and a mother who were close to you. Her response was, "They are just fine with their mother. You can just come and visit once a year." She went to add that you were both now Syrian citizens and that she was putting you in school over there and that, according to Syrian law, the mother has custody over the kids until age fifteen. I explained to her that what she was doing was not healthy for our girls and that they needed their father, but to top things off, she said that even at age fifteen, it was not guaranteed that you would return to me. She said that she had appointed your grandmother to take care of you and your sister at that time.

I was furious about that; I could not bear it any longer. My heart was about to burst from all this evil-mindedness. "You still have time to do the right thing," I told her. "You can get on an airplane today and just come home. Please! Otherwise, I have to proceed with going through the court system here in America."

"I could care less," your mother told me. "I know the laws and I am not coming back."

On September 20, I went to court after a numerous attempts to make your mother change her mind. The judge gave me a date for both your mother and me to appear in court. I sent the documents to your mother in Syria, and that was another opportunity for her to come back and do the right thing the legal way. She received the documents, reluctantly, after three attempts to serve her. On the date she was to appear in court, she did not.

So the judge gave me temporary full custody of you and your sister, which meant I could then legally proceed with getting you back. But it also gave your mother another month to come to America and talk to the judge to get shared custody if she wanted. She did not show up again.

Meanwhile, I needed a lawyer in Syria. Someone recommended a lawyer there, and after talking with him and sharing my story, he apologized for not being able to help me because he knew your mother's aunt and it would not be in his interest to represent me. Your mother's aunt was a Congresswoman in the House of Representatives in Syria at that time. She supposedly she had some influence over certain people.

I then talked with another lawyer but he was connected to the first one and would not represent me either. Finally, I found a lawyer to handle my paperwork in Syria before I arrived. At that time your mother was doing everything in her power, right or wrong, legal and illegal, to keep me from talking to you or seeing you, if and when I got there. She told me that even if I went to Syria, the only way she would let me see you both was in some designated area, guarded by police, and that I could only see you for an hour and then I would have to leave. She was the most insensitive

I had seen her thus far, that she would use you to hurt me, as though you were some pawns on a chess board. She was being irrational and I was very worried about you both.

It was now around the end of November and I still did not have permission to go to Syria. So, one day, I was talking with my older brother here in America, and he said that he was thinking of going to Syria to see his son and that maybe we could both go together. I said it was a great idea and that I would get us two tickets.

I called a travel agent and purchased two tickets for December 6, 2010. By then it was the end of November, and still I didn't have my documents. So I told your uncle to go ahead and leave without me and, maybe, when he got there, he could go to the Syrian Embassy in Syria and see why they had not approved my Visa to go there.

Wings of an Eagle

I wish I was an eagle, and fly when I please
No cage all around me, and no one to appease
I would swoop down and carry you back home
And build for you a castle, where playfully you'd roam
I would flap my sturdy wings and clear every cloud
And make for your enemies, a godforsaken shroud
I would fly to the heavens and command every star
To shine your every darkness and erase every scar
I would battle every creature I see along the way
And fight for your freedom, till my dying day.

Chapter 5

I postponed my flight for another week and waited for your uncle to resolve my issues in Syria. He finally called and said that there were some complications and that he was working on it. Then it was time for me to leave, on the 13th of December, and still I didn't have documents. I decided to go anyway. I could not wait any longer; I just needed see you and your sister. I packed my bags with Christmas presents for both of you and my sisters and relatives. It had been ten years since I had been back to Syria. I had wanted to go back and visit old friends and family, but not like this. I was not sure how I would be received or what they might think of me, with what your mother was doing. I don't usually give too much attention to what people think, but in Syria it's different. People hold you to different standards there than they do in America. Divorce in not as common as it is here. And marital problems are usually kept in the dark.

A week before leaving for Syria, I had been working on a plan to somehow get you out of the country. I needed passports for you, but your mother had taken those and all of your important documents with her. She knew she was not going to come back, she planned it that way. So I tried to get replacement passports for you and could not. It seems that in order to get passports for minors, you need the consent of both parents and the children must be present. That was going to be a big problem since you were both in another country.

Someone suggested that I might be able to obtain fake passports somewhere in Los Angeles. And while the thought of doing something illegal had never entered my mind before, I was desperate and decided to check into it. I needed passport photos of you and your sister, and, suddenly, I thought of the photo studio that had taken recent pictures of you both prior to you leaving. I went there to see if I could get copies. The clerk behind the counter searched my order history and was able to retrieve duplicates. I was ecstatic. I set out to Los Angeles to meet with someone who specialized in this illegal practice, but when I got there, I could not go through with it. I did not feel good about it and dismissed the whole idea.

I thought that maybe I could go to Syria and convince your mother, face to face, to come back. A few days before I was scheduled to leave for Syria, my lawyer in America called me with some good news. He said that the judge had granted me full custody and now I did not need your mother's approval or consent to apply for passports or other documents, I could do it all by myself. However, I still needed both of you to be present with me. Nonetheless, I was very happy about that news. *I now have the upper hand*, I thought, *and your mother does not yet know of the news.*

My mind raced to come up with a plan upon my arrival in Syria. I would have to find a way to take you and your sister to the U.S. Embassy in Syria and apply for passports there. But how was I going to do that when your mother was not going to let me see you without police supervision? I would have to think about that on the flight to Syria. I was confirmed to fly on December 13, 2010.

I boarded the plane and set out to Syria. I was thinking about a million things. I was replaying the events in my head and was hoping that this whole thing was nothing but a nightmare and hoping that soon it would all be behind me. Maybe I'd get there and things would be different. I would do anything, and agree to issues that your mother might have, just long enough to convince her to return to America and then deal with our marriage issues there. I was thinking of the dog that I had bought you as a surprise about a week after you had left for Syria. I thought of how you might have been surprised and how much you and your sister would have loved it. I had also decorated your bedroom with new furniture that I custom painted for days so that it matched your new room. I did the same for your sister's room and our bedroom. I was working night and day, trying to finish before you returned. But all of that just quickly passed through my mind, and I began to focus on the day I would arrive in Syria and see you and your sister. I had missed you terribly. I could hardly wait to hold you both in my arms and take you back home.

A couple of months after you left for Syria, I had begun to write poetry that, for some reason, made me feel better. Somehow, writing my feelings down on paper seemed to clear my head and, at the same time, release the anger that had built in my heart towards your mother. I also began to read the Bible a little more. *Maybe I can write some poems on the way to Syria to kill some time,* I thought. But I was not really in the mood for all of that.

I began to think about what I would tell you, what I would have to say to comfort you once I got a chance to see you and your sister. *What if I am not able to bring you back? How am I going to live with you being so far away?* And the thought of being away from you for fifteen years just made me sick to my stomach. I had been trying to quit smoking for a while, but I couldn't help it, I bought a pack of cigarettes at the airport. But I also took with me plenty of Nicorettes, which is a gum to help you quit smoking. So I popped one in my mouth and started chewing. It was a long flight and I had a lot to think about.

You had now been gone for six months and I had missed you every hour and every day of that long six months. As I sat staring out the window of that giant airplane, a thousand images filled my head. I was trying to be positive and optimistic and hopeful that things would work out when I got there. But negative, hateful and angry thoughts dominated my mind. I found myself thinking for hours of nothing but evil for evil. I began with a scene, possibly from some Arab Bedouin movie I had watched, where an angry hero was riding a black horse, wielding a sword, and headed toward his enemies. I felt my blood boiling with anger towards your mother and her family. I imagined me on that horse as I rode through that desert town of Alhafar where they all live and striking each one of them with my blade until everyone who had a hand in this crime was dead.

My mind returned quickly to the Bible and what I had been reading for the last few months to help me cope with this anger. I was reminded of the book of Job (*ayyoub*), in the Old Testament of the Bible, whom God had tested with so many inflictions of pain and suffering. The book slowly became my favorite book. I thought of the things God had put him through and tried to feel good about my situation. I kept thinking that there were other people in the world with a lot bigger problems than mine. I thought of the positive things about my life and found many blessings I was thankful for. I was blessed with two beautiful and healthy girls. I was thankful for the great life God had provided me with to share with my children.

I thought of the happy moments you and I had shared, from the day you were born to this day, and thought of the day when your little sister was born. How you were so jealous of having someone new to take some Daddy time away from you. But soon you became so protective and sweet and loving towards her and, later, the three of us were inseparable.

I had to make a real effort to control my every thought, one by one. Otherwise, my mind would automatically drift to thinking about the terrible things your mother and her evil family had done to me and my children, recently and in the past. I had done everything in my power to help her family, especially her brothers. I never said no to anything your mother or her family wanted. They all betrayed my trust and completely disregarded and denied all the things I had done for them. They used to love the ground I walked on. Was it all just lies? Was it just all bull shit? They were very convincing and I had been a fool to believe it. I put up with so much garbage from your mother and her family and never complained, because I didn't want to hurt your mother's feelings.

I decided I would just take it and move on. I was bigger than to be a complainer or even to confront anyone. I thought that I could handle it and avoid any drama. I kept thinking about your grandfather in Syria and the time I called for a week straight to talk to you and your sister. He finally answered the phone. "Never call her again," he told me. "Just leave your daughters and your wife alone."

This evil and heartless family was like none I had ever met or heard of in all my life. What planet were these people from to think that a father was simply going to just lie down and forget about his two daughters and not go to war with the whole world to fight for them? I guess I can understand that, from his point of view, it was not so important. Your mother had told me over the years how he had left them to fend for themselves when he decided to travel to Saudi Arabia when your mother was only six years old. He stayed there for years and would only visit them once a year, if that. How could he understand what I was going through or the pain of having your whole world just pulled from under you? And how could your mother, having gone through this feeling with her own father, do the same thing to you and your sister.

I began to pray to God to give me patience, wisdom and understanding. And help me to be forgiving. I guess the one thing that made me get through this ordeal, day after day, was the hope that God was in control and that He was going to give me justice and teach these people a lesson in humanity.

It is hard for me to share these things with you about your mother and her family. I can imagine that it is going to be hard for you to read about this. After all, it's not easy to hear anything negative about anyone's mother. I understand that and I'm sorry that I feel this way and I'm sorry things had to reach this level.

Sometimes I try to just picture your mother at her best. When she was more affectionate towards me and how sweet she was at times. She was not always like this. She was more sensitive and more caring and I loved her. So you can imagine how hard it was for me to lose her as my wife and, even worse, to lose you and your sister. I'm not a hateful person or a vindictive one either, nor have ever been. I don't hold grudges towards anyone and I am the first to forgive, always. I pray that God softens my heart towards her and her family, if only for your sake.

Chapter 6

The flight to Syria was coming to an end. I landed in France and I would see you and your sister in about twenty-four hours, hopefully. I was a little worried as I boarded the airplane from France to Damascus. What would I do if I was detained, who would I call, who had connections in the country that I could count on? What if I went to jail or, even worse, what if they made me serve in the military? How would I live with myself, knowing that I was not able to be there for you when you needed me the most? I tried to just think about you both and to think more positively.

I arrived at the Damascus airport with my heart in my stomach. I was feeling sick and anxious. This was the first time I had been back to Syria since that dreaded day I came to visit ten years earlier. I walked up to the check-in window where the attendant asked to see my passport. Upon inspection of the passport, he found that I had been away for a while and asked to see my military exempt form. He was very suspicious and kept looking at my American passport and miscellaneous documents. He asked me many questions about what I was doing in the country. He asked about where I was going to be staying while I was there and for how long. I must have been acting strangely, because he gathered my things and was about to go to see someone. I was uneasy and was expecting the worst. Just as he started to leave, a man wearing police uniform walked by me and whispered my name. I motioned to him and he came over to me.

"Don't say a word," he warned me. "I've taken the necessary steps to insure that you have no problems." He then waited for the attendant to come back and told him to go ahead and let me through. I realized then that someone had sent him to look out for me. I followed him then went to get my bags, where I was met by my brother and one of his in-laws. I later found out that the in-law was the man who sent the policeman to get me. Then we were on the way to Homs, where I would spend the night at your uncle's house and, hopefully, see you and your sister the next day.

I had missed being in Syria. I've always been in love with the idea that I was born there. It's my second home. I love the people there. They are so friendly and hospitable. They all make you feel like you are their son. On this trip I noticed the streets were clean and, as far as the eye could see on the stretch of highway we were driving on, giant, well-decorated streetlights lit the beautiful clear skies. *It is different here than what we are used to in America*, I thought. *It is slow-paced and people truly enjoy their lives.* I had always been told to visit around Christmas time. There was no harvest to deal with or much work to be done. Most people stayed indoors, visiting and playing cards.

As we approached the city of Homs, I could see the streets lit up with Christmas decorations, and I was a little surprised. Syria is a country that is predominantly Muslim, yet it feels like you are in a European country. I imagine that they are influenced by the new age of media.

I woke up the next day, the 15th of December 2010, and I called your mother to tell her that I was in Syria.

"*Hamdilla al salami,*" (Thank god for your safe arrival) she said in a cold manner and then she said that she couldn't talk until after 4pm. I was so anxious to see you and now I'd have to wait for most of the day. Finally I talked with your mom again and she said that if I wanted to see you, I would have to meet her at the Mutranieh church, or as it is officially known, "Umm Al Zinnar," meaning the church of our Virgin Lady.

That is where I would only see you for an hour under supervision. She was kind enough to choose a place that was not guarded by police. She made sure to remind me of that. I should be so grateful. She made it seem like she was doing me a favor. I was very upset about that, even though I was expecting it. I had waited six months to see you and now she wouldn't let me see you at my own house. It was very disappointing. But I agreed, and the same night I met you and your sister there and was thrilled.

You were very happy to see me but did not greet me in the same way as you used to when we were in America. I used to come home, and the minute you heard the keys clanging, you and your sister would rush to the door yelling, "Daddy, Daddy. Daddy is home." Then you would give me hugs and kisses. I understood; there was concern in your eyes and I knew you needed answers.

Your mother brought you over. She just shook my hand like I was a business man she had never met and we entered an office the size of 3x3 meters. I was asked to hand over my passport as a security deposit, just in case I was going to run away with you or something. It was very embarrassing for me, but I handed over my passport and Identification. The Deacon took my papers and went up the stairs to hand them to the Archbishop in charge of the church. When he came back, he had me sign an agreement that was in Arabic. He explained it was my visitation rights.

There we were. Me, you, your sister, and some church deacon watching over us. I was very uncomfortable. I never thought in a million years that this would ever happen to me. I had read and heard about it happening to other people, but to me, it was unacceptable. There you both were, in front of me, and I felt like a guest you were visiting with. I looked at the clock on the wall and I realized that I should be telling you something since the minutes were ticking away. I did not know if I should tell you what was happening to our family, not knowing whether this deacon was on your mom's side or not.

She had, after all, called him by his first name, so I didn't want to say much except how much I missed you and try to gather as many hugs and kisses as you would give me. I spent about an hour and then your mom came back to pick you up. I was heartbroken. *Is this the way it is going to be?* I asked myself. Nevertheless, I enjoyed it very much. I couldn't stop hugging and kissing you. You looked so good and your Arabic was really impressive. You did not speak to me in English nor did your sister. I was glad but worried that you might forget the English language.

When your mom picked you up, I asked for my passport and ID back. Your sister said, "Daddy, come with us." I wanted to cry but held it until you were out of sight. I told your mother that I would see you both the next day and we would talk.

The next day I contacted my attorney in Syria and met with him to figure out what my rights were there and also to sign an agreement making him officially my attorney to represent me in the church hearings led by the Archbishop. He told me what my rights were and explained that I could only see you and your sister for two hours every other day or so, according to the specific laws set forth by the Archbishop. I was also told that your mother was not obligated to allow me the freedom of being with you overnight at my own place. It made me very upset that your mom would treat me like a stranger and not let me see you freely.

I instructed my attorney to do everything in his power to get me more time with you. I went back home and began to look at my options.

First, I needed to assure my legal status in Syria. So the attorney and I went from office to office trying to get a document that gave me the right to visit the country. We had a connection at city hall, and with a little bribe, the man assured me that the matter was resolved and not to worry. That man would come in handy later.

Now every day revolved around 6pm. That is when I would see you at the church and your mom would then pick you up at 8pm. Again, like the same old routine, I would hand the guy my passport and identification and I would spend quality time with you, playing with your new toys that I bought for you in America.

You seemed to be okay with us meeting there, as though you understood the program, but I knew you better. You are good at hiding your true emotions and you seemed so strong, I thought. Your sister, on the other hand, wanted to go to my house and would voice that, saying," Baba, let's go to your house and play there," and it would bring tears to my eyes, hearing that, 'Your house.' It felt as though we were not a family anymore. But I would just hold her and change the subject quickly.

For a few days I would talk briefly with your mother. The rest of the time, she told me that her lawyer and my lawyer should communicate with each other so that we could just get a court date with the Archbishop. I decided to call someone who I had met and admired when I got married here years ago. That man was your mother's uncle. I also called my cousin Zuhair. He is a second cousin who my dad had much respect for and, once before he passed away, told me about.

I called Zuhair and explained that I needed him to be present with me to speak with the Archbishop before any official hearings between me and your mother. And that I wanted your mom and her uncle there, too. I thought that perhaps a peaceful solution might come from family members.

We set the meeting and everyone showed up. Now we each had to explain to the *Mutran* (Archbishop) our side of the story and see if we could resolve things without going through the courts. I shared with everyone the way we lived in America and what a nice life I had provided for my wife and my children. I expressed my concerns for you and your sister and told them that your mother had deceived me by pretending to come to Syria strictly for a short visit and then decided not to return to America.

The Archbishop asked me if I wanted her back and I said, yes. I would forgive her and we could all go back to America. Of course at the time, my lips were speaking what my heart was not feeling.

Your mother began to speak and before long she was losing credibility with everyone there. Even her uncle, who she brought for support, was having a hard time believing things she said. They all knew me and my reputation and had heard all the wonderful things about me from your mother and her parents for years prior to this incident.

Her uncle stepped up and asked her a simple and wise question. "How is it," he asked, "that for the last few years that you've been married and came back to Syria several times telling us about your life with your husband being a fairy tale and how he is the man of your dreams and that he was like your brother, father and husband and meant the world to you, and now you say just the opposite?"

Your mother realized that she was not reaching anyone or gaining any support and asked to be excused. "This is my life," she said, "and I do not wish to be with this person."

This person. Wow, I knew at that point that she had made up her mind and there was no changing it. The meeting was over and nothing was accomplished; as a matter of fact, it got worse.

Clear Blue Sky

Lord won't you help me I'm falling behind
My heart is aching and my eyes are blind
I travel on a road forsaken by
Some peace and joy and clear blue sky
My feet are bleeding from thorns and glass
And there are so many mountains and valleys to pass
The thunder all around me is loud and clear
But it does not compare to the crying I hear
I feel rage and anger way deep in my bones
Consuming the love and compassion I've known
Won't you ease my mind and comfort my soul
This wickedness comes through no fault of my own
I was born from the ashes, and to the ashes I'll return
But I fear my soul will forever burn
I ask your forgiveness, please hear my call
In the name of Jesus, the Sheppard of all

Chapter 7

Christmas was slowly approaching and I had wrapped all of your gifts. I was hopeful that your mother would allow you to spend Christmas at my house, as opposed to that confined space in church. Many thoughts came to mind that interrupted my holiday spirit. I thought that if she really wanted to make a statement, this would be her opportunity to shine. I bet she was thinking of keeping you away from me, but in the back of her mind, she was probably fearing what relatives might say. She is cleaver that way. She may want to play the nice and caring card around the holiday to show everyone how thoughtful she is towards her girls. Boy, can she put on a show when she wants to.

Meanwhile, I was getting nothing but bad news from my lawyer regarding the hearings there in Syria. He told me that it was literally impossible to win the case. And even though I had official court orders from America, they were of no use in Syria. Your mother, potentially, had the right to keep you in Syria until the age of fifteen or possibly eighteen. I had to think of some other way to take you back to America.

I went online to research the borders of Syria and tried to find a way I could drive you to a neighboring country and then fly you to America. It sounded easy in theory, but according to my lawyer, your mother had placed your names as restricted from traveling through any border. And she also had the church place my name on a similar list. She did this to insure I would not leave the country without going to court. I was furious about that. That was one of the lowest things I had seen her do so far, but I had a feeling that it would not be the last.

It turned out that she was asking for a ridiculous amount of money, based on her lawyer's papers that my attorney forwarded to me. An amount I did not have. Not that money was of any importance, but it showed me a different side of your mother. Money has never been as important to me as having a happy home and a happy marriage and a happy family.

I asked my attorney to respond by offering her all the money I had and all that I possessed if she would return to America with you and your sister, but she insisted that was never going to happen. It was either agree to her demands, or visiting with you would become difficult. That felt like blackmail, greed and selfishness. At that point, reality set in and I realized that I was dealing with a more serious problem than what I had anticipated. I had to do something.

I was looking for an internet café, walking around in the city of Homs where your mother and you currently resided. I found one and began to do some research at the U.S. Embassy's website to see if they would be of any help. I found that in order to talk to them, I would have to set up an appointment, online only. I thought maybe if I were to provide them with the court order from America, they might be able to issue me some new passports for you and your sister. And if I was to find a way for us to travel outside of Syria, having passports would be essential.

I began to search for an available appointment and was shocked to find that in the whole month of December there were only three appointments available. The 26th, the 27th, and the 28th. So I went to January's appointment calendar and there were none available for that month. That was a problem since I was scheduled to leave Syria on the 20th of January. I only had those three days in December to make the appointment. I moved quickly and filled each day with an appointment, just in case I was not able to be with you on one of those days.

On the 24th of December, I called your mother and asked if it would be okay for me to be with you for Christmas Eve, since it was my birthday the following day. I could not believe I was actually asking such a question. But I had to be nice in order to gain her trust. She said that she would meet me at the church that day and I could have you both spend the night but to return with you the next evening. I was a bit surprised, but I had my doubts about her intentions. I was sure there was something behind that sudden spurt of compassion.

My heart was pounding because one of the appointments with the Embassy was on the 26th, and I needed to convince your mother to let you both spend two nights with me so that, maybe, I could take you to Damascus and try to get the passports.

I met you at the church, hoping that they would forget to ask for my passport as collateral because I needed it to show the Embassy proof of who I was. But, no such luck. The deacon at the church asked me for it right away, as well as for my California ID. And your mother did not agree to my plea to have you stay with me longer than one day.

At last I had you all to myself. Wow, what a great feeling. I could not believe it. Finally after six months, I was now able to really hold you and play with you without looking at a clock. I held hands with both of you. We walked down the street from the church and found a photography studio. And, as normal as this may sound, taking a photograph with you made me a little nervous. I was thinking one step ahead and needed to have passport photos, which would be necessary to obtain passports later. I walked in and had the lady take some pictures of us for Christmas, just in case you told your mother. I asked the lady not to mention anything about passports or travel while she snapped the photos I needed.

We had a great time opening presents, and you both loved everything I brought for you from America. We watched movies and ate together, but my mind was on the appointment. What would I have to do? Should I miss the appointment and see if I could talk your mother into allowing me to have you again the following day? I would just have to wait and see.

Spending Christmas morning with you was incredible. We had a lot of fun. We ate cereal and played with more toys. But I had to take you back to your mother and miss out on our first appointment that was set for the following day. I took a taxi back to the church to meet your mother; I was very nice to her and told her how much fun we had. "Can I have them both spend the night again tomorrow?" I asked.

"No," she said. She wanted to spend some time with you but said that I could pick you up on the 27th in the afternoon to spend the night and have you back on the 28th at five that evening. My second appointment was at nine in the morning on the 27th, so that meant a second missed appointment.

The 27th of December I went to the church and met you there at 3pm. I was very nervous because I knew that it is my final chance to take you to Damascus to try to get your passports. I did not waste any time. I took you both home. Then I needed to get to Damascus as soon as possible so that we could make the last appointment the next day at eight in the morning. I was reluctant to tell your uncle Nick about what I was doing because he was very open when it came to sharing information. But I had no choice; I had to tell someone, just in case something went wrong.

I took him aside and explained that I was going to take you and your sister to Damascus and spend some time at an amusement park called the Ski Mall. I had to come up with something fun so that you were both excited to go and keep you interested. You both loved the idea.

Your uncle insisted on going with us because he knew some people there and said that they might help us with directions in Damascus. I reluctantly agreed, but told him to keep it quiet, due to the fact that I had signed a visitation agreement that restricted me from traveling with you outside the city of Homs. I decided to drive myself, and in a matter of fifteen minutes we got ready and off we went.

It was around 5pm and it would take over two hours to get from Homs to Damascus. However, I did not tell you that it was Damascus we were going to; I just said that the amusement park was a little far away. My heart was pounding as though I was stealing something or running away from someone. All the way there I was hoping that your mother would not call us. For all she knew, we were still in Homs.

We finally got to Damascus. You were looking outside the window and asked me, "Baba, where are we?"

I lied and said we are in Homs.

"Baba, this is not Homs," you said, "this is Damascus."

I looked at your uncle in disbelief. "How do you know that this is Damascus," I asked?

"The mosques in Damascus have different colors than the ones in Homs," you replied,

We met with your uncle's in-laws. I needed to take you to the Mall before it closed so that my story would check out in case someone found out that we drove outside of Homs.

So far not even your uncle knew what I had in mind for the next day. I was nervous visiting there at his In-law's house. It was then around 7pm and I needed to take you to the Mall, even if for just one hour. As I was thinking of my next move and listening to the guests talking about nothing at all, I got the most dreaded phone call on my cell phone. I could see on the screen that it was your mother. Should I answer or should I just let it ring? If I let it ring, she might get suspicious, so I excused myself and went outside to talk with her.

I told her that everything was fine and that you and your sister were fine, too. She asked to speak to you, but I knew that if she asked where you were, you might tell her that we were in Damascus. So I took it upon myself to tell her. I said that we were in Damascus and that I was taking you and your sister to an amusement park and that we would be back the next day as planned. I told her that we would possibly be staying the night at my brother's in-law's.

I hadn't even finished my sentence before your mother exploded on the phone like the world just came to an end. She was yelling so loud and with much violence and profanity and threats toward me and my family. She kept saying, "You bring back my girls back this hour or else." She said that she would inform the police and reminded me that what I was doing was kidnapping.

Really, I thought. *Kidnapping*? "You are crazy and you need help" I said. "Just listen to what you are saying to me. I am still your husband and the father of your children and you threaten me? I will not be bringing them back until tomorrow afternoon by 5pm as we agreed."

She got more furious and continued with her threats. She said that she had lots of connections in Syria that could cause me a lot of trouble.

"Go ahead do whatever you want," I said. "I will not be back until tomorrow afternoon." I hung up the phone.

I went back inside the house and pulled your uncle to the side. I told him what had happened on the phone with your mother. "She is probably on her way to Damascus as we speak," I said. "I need to go to the Ski Mall quickly so that the girls can play there since I promised them that and to keep the story in check should the Archbishop get involved."

You kept asking me, "When are we going to the Ski Mall, Daddy?"

"We are going now," I said. I asked one of the men there for directions and a man by the name of Sam offered to take us. On the way there, I shared my dilemma with him about your mother and told him that I needed to stay in Damascus long enough to meet with the consulate at the U.S. Embassy the following day because they needed to see my daughters and me for an interview. I didn't want to share any more information than that with either your uncle or Sam. Sam suggested that we stay at his house and kept assuring me that no one had the right to come inside his house without a warrant, not even the police.

It took us about thirty minutes to get to the Ski Mall and Amusement park. I was watching everyone in sight very closely. Your mother would have no problem finding the place as it was one of the most famous malls in Damascus.

We found the amusement park and went inside. This place was huge. I thought that we had large malls in America, but this one was big. It had an ice skating rink in the center of the mall where many kids and their parents were learning to skate. And it housed the most famous designers from all around the world.

So far, you and your sister didn't know what was going on. We played all kinds of games in the biggest arcade I've ever seen. My heart was racing and all I wanted to do at that point was get on our way. I was satisfied that I came through on my promise to take you there and now we must go. You and your sister were hungry and even though we were pressed for time, I decided to get some food and take a moment to think about our next step.

It had been about an hour and a half since I last spoke with your mother. If she was thinking of driving to Damascus, she would probably have made it already. She was calling my cell phone, but I didn't answer. My phone was ringing off the hook with so many people calling me. You would think that the world was coming to an end.

I finally got a phone call from my cousin Zouher. He was now officially my sponsor and the mediator between your mother and me. She had called and asked him to talk to me. I answered his call. He explained that your mother had called him and asked him to inform me about the laws there in Syria and to bring you both back to Homs immediately. I said that what she was doing was wrong and that I would bring my daughters back by 5 pm the next day. I assured him that I had a lot of respect for him and that I would not risk his reputation. I also expressed to him that what your mother was doing was shameful. The way that she was talking to me was unacceptable and I had as much right to be with my daughters as she did. I told him that I would not be back that day under any circumstance.

As I got off the phone, I noticed that your Uncle Nick was talking to someone on his cell phone with a loud voice. I heard him tell that person our current location. That made me very angry, especially after I had told him how sensitive our situation was. I made him get off the phone and I quickly found a little restaurant on the second floor where I could observe who was coming into the mall. I noticed a lot of strange looks directed at us. We placed our food order and made sure it would come quickly. I had a moment to take you both to the restroom. When we came back, our food was ready. I could hardly eat a bite, but I enjoyed watching you both.

I grabbed both of you by the hand and we slowly walked down the stairs to leave. I was still thinking that maybe someone outside might be waiting for us. I told Sam to get the car and meet us at the door. He did. We got in the car and drove off. From the backseat I was watching to see if we were being followed. We were not.

It was getting late and I was getting so much pressure from your uncle and Sam to just return to Sam's house, but I insisted that I wanted to go to a hotel that was close to the U.S. Embassy. I instructed your uncle and Sam to drop us off at the hotel and then go home.

Sam used his name to get us a hotel room at what seemed to be a nice hotel. I told them that, if they should have any contact with your mother, to deny our whereabouts and to meet us at the hotel the following morning.

Moments later we went to our room, where I tried to think about my next move. I unplugged the phone and turned my cell phone off. I found you to be a little suspicious, asking me why we were staying at a hotel. I said that I wanted to spend some time with you and your sister alone. It was so comforting to finally be able to relax and not feel like we were on the run – even though we were.

We started to play and jump on the beds together and before long I moved the two single beds together and told you a couple of your favorite bedtime stories about the three little pigs and the wolf. And before long, you both fell asleep. I just sat there watching you both and wondering if I was going to pull this thing off in the morning. I just hoped that your uncle and Sam were not going to be followed when they picked us up in the morning. I was so exhausted; I just fell asleep in between the both of you.

The next morning I woke up early at five, feeling tired and stressed out. I went to take a shower and get ready. I turned the water on and brown water came out. I just shook my head but managed to still take a shower. I woke you both up, and while we were getting ready, I heard a knock at the door that startled me a little. I looked at the time – it was seven o'clock.

"Who is it?" I asked.

"Open the door, it's Sam," I heard Sam say from the hallway.

"Did anyone follow you?" I asked.

"No," he said.

We all walked down the stairs and had to wait in the lobby of the hotel until they checked the room and only then we could leave. It took so long and I was getting anxious.

Your uncle began to tell me about the events that took place the night before when he and Sam arrived at the house. He said that your mother contacted them and was adamant about knowing where I was and where I had taken you. She had driven with her cousin and some off duty policeman to Damascus in search of us. They told her what I instructed them to tell her: nothing at all. She supposedly tried to threaten them with bringing the police to their house if they did not tell her where I was. But that did not faze them and they told her that being with my daughters was not illegal since there were no court papers she could provide to have you taken from me. Still they were not able to convince her to just go back to Homs.

After a lot of talk on the phone, Sam convinced her and her friends to meet with him. After they met and talked for a few minutes, she was still not convinced, even though the policeman who was with her told her that I wasn't doing anything wrong, that I was just spending time with my girls. Anyway, your uncle told me that she was very disrespectful towards him and our whole family. They did not know whether she stayed in Damascus or went back that same night to Homs.

Still at the hotel, there was a strange Asian man taking pictures next to us and he kept looking at you and your sister. I did not know what to think of him. He then approached you and wanted to take a picture with both of you. I didn't like that. I watched him closely and told him that you did not like to take pictures, but he continued to come close. I grabbed you both and sat you down next to me as he just smiled and left. I was thinking, what a wreck I was to suspect even an Asian tourist. A few minutes later our room was inspected and we were on our way.

Chapter 8

On the way to the Embassy, Sam asked me to pay attention to the plain-clothed secret service men who were placed on every corner of every street. They were all properly dressed to hide an automatic machine gun. Sam and your uncle dropped us off at the doorsteps of the U.S. Embassy, where armed guards were everywhere. Strangely, I felt safer as they drove off.

Before entering the Embassy, the guard asked if I had an appointment. "Yes," I said. He looked on his appointment book and found my name. He asked me for my passport, as I knew he would. I explained to him that the church had possession of it and that they also had my California ID. He said that he would not be able to let me in unless I provided some ID. I looked in my wallet to show him a credit card, but he was not pleased with that since it did not have my picture on it. As I was looking in my wallet, I was shocked to see an expired license still in the wallet which I did not know I had and I showed him that. After pleading my case and telling him how important it was for me to meet with the consulate, he let me in. I was very thankful for that.

We finally got to the window where we were to meet with a counselor regarding our situation. I told him the story of you and your sister and how your mother had taken you from America and refused to take you back. I explained that I needed his help to apply for new passports. He said that he would need the mother to be present. I showed him the court papers from America that gave me sole custody of both of you and explained to him that with sole custody the court told me that I would not need the mother's permission. He inspected them and said that while these documents were issued to me, they meant nothing in Syria. I pleaded with him and told him that I was in a desperate situation and that he was the only person I could turn to. He said that he needed to talk with a supervisor.

A few minutes later he came back and said that we could try to apply for the passports, but first he had to run it by the State Department in Washington, DC and, even then, it was not a 100% guarantee that the passports would be issued.

He asked for your photos that I had taken with you in Homs a few days earlier. He mentioned the fact that we had missed two previous appointments and asked about that. I just said that we had transportation issues. He was very helpful and then sent us outside to wait for the supervisor.

After waiting for over an hour, the supervisor called us into his office where I had to convince him that we were American citizens and we needed these passports in order to be able to leave the country. He gave me some warnings about trying to leave Syria and said that it was going to be dangerous for me to try leaving through any border, especially the Lebanese border. And that I needed to be sure before trying. And furthermore, if I were to get caught, the United States would not be able to help me due to the fact that this was a civil matter in Syria. He said that he was not able to approve my request until he contacted the State Department in America and he would then let me know by phone in a few days whether or not he would issue new passports.

I was so relieved to have been able to do this and now it was just a waiting game. I gave you a big hug even though you did not know why. Now I just needed to get on the road quickly and get to Homs by 5pm that day as I had promised. On the way home your uncle asked if the Embassy was able to help me. "No, no luck," I said. I did not want him to know any more sensitive information from that point on.

We got to Homs at around 5pm and went straight to the church where Zouher and your mother's cousin were waiting. I talked to them for a few minutes and then they took you both to your mother's. Needless to say, from then on it was going to be difficult for me to see you. I was not able to take you with me to your uncle's house so that we could spend more time together. Your mother did not allow me to be with you alone after that incident.

From then on it was strictly at the church, and to make things worse, she brought her own guard to stay with us while I visited with you. Her uncle started coming as additional guard. While it was uncomfortable, it was better than nothing. However, her uncle had a heart unlike the rest of your mother's family. He knew how much I loved my girls by the way I was playing with you on the floor of that little office and he told me that the next time I needed to see you, it would be okay to do it at his house. And sure enough, a week later I met you there. Unfortunately, it was the time when I had to say goodbye. It was the most difficult thing I've ever had to do.

That day was very emotional for all of us. The look on your faces made me hate myself for somehow letting your mom do this to our family. And then your sister took ahold of my neck and would not let go, as if she felt I was not coming back. She was crying and screaming and my tears were like waterfalls from behind my sunglasses. I was trying not to show you that side of me, but after a lot of help from the uncle, she finally let me go and continued to cry. I had to go, but my heart was shattered into a million pieces. I walked down the street while you both were watching me walk away from the third floor balcony. The look on your face, I will never forget. You broke my heart with a look that will be imbedded in my eyes forever. I could not believe what was happening. I felt helpless. *Is this really happening? Am I about to leave my daughters behind in this country?*

After leaving the uncle's house, I was getting ready to leave Syria the next day. Before leaving, I stopped by the church and gave the Archbishop enough money to give to your mother on a monthly basis and to get a release from him allowing me to leave the country legally. He gave me my passport and ID and I left.

I went to Alfouhila to say goodbye to your aunts and the rest of the relatives. It was also very emotional, but we managed. They were trying very hard to console me by saying that I did the best I could do and that I had to face the facts and begin to accept this as my fate. I'm not sure if anyone understood the way I was feeling. To just come all this way and go back to America empty-handed was nothing short of total failure in my eyes.

About 4pm that day I received a phone call that would change things. It was the man from the U.S. Embassy; he said that my request was approved and that I could pick up your new passports the next day. I was on cloud nine but kept it to myself.

The next day I left for the Damascus airport a little earlier than necessary so that I could stop by and collect the passports. Now I felt better. *I'll be better prepared the next time,* I thought. And hopefully it wouldn't be long when I'd come back to Syria with a plan to get you out.

Chapter 9

A couple of days later I was back in America and back to work. Everyone was asking me about what happened, but I just said that my girls were healthy and seemed happy and that was all that mattered. I did not share the details with anyone. And for the next few days, I would just be at home, alone, thinking of what to do next. I would replay the events that took place while I was in Syria over and over in my head and try to see where I went wrong.

Your mother had had many things to say to the judge during the first hearing in Syria. He was not just a judge but also the Archbishop or *Mutran*. The assistant to the *Mutran* was writing everything down word for word which, by the way, is evidence that everything I'm sharing with you can be verified, but I'm sure that you do not doubt me.

Your mom initially told the *Mutran* that the reason she went back to Syria and wanted a divorce was because I stopped loving her and that I did not speak sweet words to her. That, in itself, did not get her much sympathy. He told her that many marriages go through dry spells, but that was not a valid reason to break up a family.

She then shifted her story so that it was more dramatic and said that I had once beaten her, which was a lie. On our first date in an internet café, the subject had been about the type of husband she was attracted to. I was very straight-forward with her about who I was and what my qualities were. I shared with her what I stood for and what I was against. I remember that I told her that very clearly. I said that a man who lays a finger on a woman as to harm her, no matter the circumstance, was no man at all, but a coward. I believed that then and still do to this date.

I think that your mother's attorney told her to say those false accusations in order to make the case more dramatic and also to be able to ask for a divorce and collect money. Otherwise, no one was going to take her seriously. So she lied about me to my face and in front of God.

She was capable of saying anything because she was no longer the person I knew. It seemed like she was on stage, acting this part, with no regard to what implications it had on me or my children.

She had lost so much weight by then. And I was worried about her health. I tried to whisper to her as she stood there in court next to some scum lawyer to just stop with all the lies, but she just continued. That's when I knew that it was over between us. We had been married for nine years and had two beautiful children, but she did not value any of it. I looked at her and said *"Asaftik, asaftik,"*(shame on you) what have you done? We can still work things out. This is a very big decision, just think of the girls." But she just looked away. My attorney was a major disappointment at that hearing and did not object to anything that her attorney was falsely accusing me of.

I began to speak, but with my blood boiling at the lies they told, I must have sounded like a mad man. "My language here is inadequate to defend myself," I told her attorney, "but if we were in America, my attorney there would eat you for breakfast and shit you out for lunch." I then simply walked out and that was the last time I saw her that trip.

Now, once again back in America, I felt as though I had at least gone to Syria and faced some of the people who had the wrong idea about me and your mother. I believe that I set the record straight and I was very confident that they saw the same man who they had known for so many years.

I was comforted by the fact that you and your sister seemed happy in Syria. You had mentioned to me how much you liked it there with your new friends. I don't know how much your mother influenced your mentality, but I do know that you were being fed indirectly a lot of wrong and hurtful information from your mother and her family.

For example, the first day I met you and your sister in Syria at the church, the first thing you asked me was, "Is it true that you and Uncle Nick are coming to kidnap us and take us back to America?"

I was shocked to hear that and I knew that was not something you would come up with on your own. You must have heard someone say that, because you loved your uncle, he was your favorite. I assured you that we were not there to do that and that I loved you both very much.

Secondly, you were afraid all night when you spent the first night with me; you asked if we could stay up all night until morning. I didn't know why at that time, but you were scared that someone was going to take you away.

I stayed up with you as long as I could until I could hardly keep my eyes open. Then you did something funny, you went to the bathroom and put water on your hands and then tried to wash my face so that I would stay up. That was funny because, when we were in America, I used to tell you that in order to stay up longer, you must wash your face and that made it feel like a new day. So you kept me up and then you started to cry, saying that you wanted to go to your mother's house. I kept telling you stories and still you did not want to go to sleep. Out of exhaustion, I think I finally passed out and so did you. In the morning, you seemed to be okay and with your normal sense of humor.

*   *   *

As I'm writing this I am wondering how old you are as you are reading this, if you are reading it at all. My life has been turned upside since you both went to Syria. I am trying to adjust, but it's been hard. Sometimes I cannot focus on anything and I have somewhat lost interest in most things that I used to enjoy with you. I sometimes feel like going fishing and I will remember the times we would go to the lake and fish, but somehow it's not the same so I just forget about going. Even going to a sushi restaurant has not been the same because you loved sushi and it now does not taste the same without you enjoying it with me.

I am trying best as I can to have a semi-normal life. But I get very emotional around any children your ages. I sometimes see a girl your age as she is riding a bike or running or laughing and my tears begin to fall. I miss the smell of your hair and your skin. I miss the small things that we used to do like waking up together and eating cereal and watching cartoons with you. I miss your cute smile and distinctive laugh. I miss just being there to answer your curious questions and playing games in the car as I drive you to school.

Chapter 10

The Second Trip to Syria

In April of 2011, violence erupted in Syria which was triggered by the beatings of a handful of children who had painted offensive graffiti about the current president. Citizens took to the streets to protest the cruel treatment of these children and the lack of freedom of speech. They found courage from neighboring countries, like Tunisia and Egypt that were also protesting against their own governments at that time.

As a result of the violence, the Syrian army also took to the streets to contain the situation and found themselves entering a more serious problem than just a demonstration. It seemed that some of the people who were demonstrating had a different agenda. They took advantage of this once-in-a-lifetime opportunity to try to overthrow the current regime. What started as a small, peaceful demonstration soon spawned similar demonstrations all around the country.

I left America for Syria in June, 2011, to share both of your birthdays. This was the second trip I would take in my attempt to bring you back. It was an incredible time. We were able to spend more time with each other on this trip, unlike the last time I was in Syria. Your mother was more willing this time to let you be with me and spend more time together. She was more comfortable in the fact that I was coming to see you twice a year and must have felt confident in the fact that I was not able to get you out.

I rented a house in a small town called Fairouzeh on the outskirts of Homs where you both were attending school. We began to sleep there and were close to Alfouhila, my home town, so we would drive there almost daily. There you both found three friends you loved and did not want to be parted from.

We held your birthday party at your Aunt Mariam's house and there we had a beautiful cake and a ton of presents and lots of great food. You were so happy and I was in heaven, just seeing you and your sister laughing and enjoying all the wonderful gifts I got for you from America.

My vacation was planned for about thirty-five days. During that time the situation in Syria was escalating and the violence was evident, as the sound of gunfire and cannons was now a way of life. We would hear the gunfire and the cannon fire just down the street. We would laugh hysterically when we heard gunfire and I would ask, "Who is farting?" This was my way of making light of a very bad and dangerous situation.

I would also try to keep you busy with games and stories until you went to sleep. I told you a seven-part story about a powerful frog and its special powers and you couldn't wait until bedtime so that you could hear another part of the story. I, too, loved telling it and watching your face light up with anticipation.

The story of the frog was inspired by a science teacher who once told me that if I attempted to place a frog in boiling water, it would jump out immediately. But if I placed it in a pot of room temperature water, it would stay there. And as I turned the heat on, the frog would continue to remain there while the water got hotter and hotter – to the point of boiling – and, ultimately, it would die in the pot.

However, the frog in the stories I was telling you would ultimately jump out before the fire consumed it and become a hero.

There had never been a better opportunity for me to find a way to get us out. I was seeing you both freely and had ample time to come up with a plan. While I was in America, I had begun to research the borders of Syria and had found that a way through neighboring Turkey was a clear choice. Since the beginning of the violence in Syria, people were escaping across the border into Turkey at a place called *Jisr Al Shighour*. The Turkish government was receiving them and helping to place them in camps along that border. So my thoughts were to get into a car and drive us there and just cross along with the thousands of people who were doing it already. I asked a friend about that and how he might help me.

His response was not what I wanted to hear. He informed me that people at that border were being shot to death as they crossed the border and that I should not gamble with our lives. However, he knew of someone who could help us cross into Turkey by a different method. He assured me that, while it may be costly, he trusted the man and it would be a safer alternative. "Here is how it works," he said. "It will cost about $15,000. The person will drive you to a destination where there is an underground tunnel that a group uses to smuggle goods into and out of Syria."

He told me that, on the other side of the tunnel, a van would be awaiting our arrival and would drive us to a nearby airport where we would fly to the capital of Turkey and from there get to the U.S. Embassy and seek help. It was full proof, he said. Either one would be a difficult decision; I was very scared of what might go wrong. Dragging two young daughters into a desert where so many things could go wrong seemed pretty dangerous.

Would we be prepared? How much danger is there? What happens if there is no one on the other side of the tunnel? How much walking is involved if we have to walk? These questions ran through my head for days.

Meanwhile, I thought of another way, through neighboring Lebanon, and contacted the U.S. Embassy in Beirut, Lebanon, to ask about that option. I was told that, while they were not able to help me to cross the border, they would receive us at the Embassy and keep us safe until we found a way out. However, they said, I must have an Exit Visa from the Syrian authorities. Otherwise, I would be stuck in Lebanon with no way to go to America and, even worse, the Lebanese authorities would have to drive me back to the Syrian border and I would have to answer to them. I was now lost and did not know what to do. The tunnel option was becoming the clear and only choice. I called my friend and told him to get started on that and to let me know the details.

Since Homs was under attack almost daily, we were not able to freely go where ever we wanted. I still had a chance to take you to one of your favorite places, *Lala Zena,* a fun arcade and restaurant there in Homs. We also had a chance to go to the local Fairouzeh swimming pool and spend some time there along with your friends, Andie, Zaina and Zoya.

But one of your favorite things we did while I was there was when we would go to the almond fields and the watermelon fields and have a contest to see who could find the biggest almond.

I showed you where I was born and where I used to play and you loved that. This trip was special and we all became very close again. We slept at your Aunt Alice's house when we were in Alfouhila, and you would wake up and go to the hen house and collect the eggs for that day. Then we would eat breakfast and go off to visit whomever was awake.

Your mother and I were still going to court and had a scheduled meeting with the church in a few days. All during this trip your mother had been cooperative and I did not know why she was being that way.

I received a call from her one day to check up on you and your sister. She said that she wanted to talk to me about a matter that would be kept secret between us. I agreed. She said that she had been thinking of letting me take you both with me to America. She said that she had decided that it would be best for her to continue to live in Syria and focus on her new career. And that the responsibility of watching over you was taking a toll on her parents. She also said that it was getting pretty dangerous there in Syria, with the violence and instability of the government. She said that she was now officially with the opposition fighting against the current regime. I was concerned about that but continued listening. She said that it was better for us to stop the court hearings and just come to a mutual agreement. This sounded too good to be true, I thought. As she continued talking, I was anxious to get to the bottom line. I assured her that whatever she felt was fair, I would agree to.

I preferred that she went with us because it was not safe there in Syria, but she said that she had a contract with her work and was not able to leave yet. Your mother was going to go home and come up with a financial agreement that would make her comfortable and she would let me know what it was. I told her that whatever amount she wanted, I was willing to pay. That same day she called me back and said that she had come up with the solution. She said that she would agree to let you go with me to America on three conditions.

First, I would have to drop the court case I had against her in America. Second, I would have to agree to a divorce. And finally, I had to give her money, in cash, before I left Syria. The amount of money she demanded was much more than I had, even if I sold everything I owned, but I agreed.

At that point, I was not cleaver to her ways and didn't think too much about it. But if that was what it took to have you and your sister back home, then so be it. I told her that whoever she trusted to receive this money should meet us at the airport where I would hand them the money, get my girls, and leave Syria that same day. How I was going to get this sum of money together did not concern me; I would find a way to borrow two hundred thousand dollars and spend my life paying it back. I was now hopeful that this whole thing would soon be behind us and we would all be in America in a few days.

She asked me what I thought of the church pastor, who was also the assistant to the Archbishop; I said that he seemed very genuine. She said that if we both agreed, he would meet with us prior to the official hearing and we could possibly resolve our issues out of court. I told her to set up the meeting and I would be there. She reminded me again to keep this as a secret between us because she was worried about what people would think if they found out. She said that they might think that she had sold her girls for money.

I just shook my head, thinking the same. But I assured her that no one would know, and if anyone asked me, I would simply say that she had let them go because, as a mother, she was concerned for their well-being.

I continued to commend her on the decision and told her that I would appreciate if she would also come visit you and your sister every chance she got.

We met with the pastor early one morning and began to discuss our issues. The pastor asked if he could intervene for a moment and ask us a few questions. He asked us both if there was a chance that we would get back together. Your mother answered first. "No," she said. Then he asked me and I also said no because, at this point, we had a secret agreement. He went on to explain himself and also told us to keep this meeting a secret. *Everything is about secrets in this country,* I thought to myself.

The pastor said that he had a lot of influence with the Archbishop, and that we could possibly resolve our issues behind closed doors rather than for both of us to continue with the court system there in Syria. He told us it could take up to seven years to get an official divorce. The thought of waiting seven more years for this ordeal to end was not an option for me. I interrupted and told him about the agreement your mother and I had made to dissolve our marriage and that I had agreed to drop the court case in America. Your mother told him that she would agree to release our girls to me based on those terms.

The pastor had a puzzled look and asked about the money demands that your mother had asked for in the hearings. Your mother simply said that she and I had come to a mutual agreement regarding that. He agreed that it would be best. I explained to him that the court papers would arrive within ten days and, at that point, we would meet again to draw up final paperwork. We all agreed.

This also came at a time where my options to gamble with our lives through tunnels was not making sense. I kept this between me and your mother; no one knew. I promised your mother that my attorney in America was working on some paperwork that would give her equal custody should she decide to go back to America in the future. My attorney was against this idea and was concerned that I was being tricked by your mother. I explained to him that I was okay with it and that I knew what I was doing. The paperwork was drawn up by my attorney in America and I instructed him to mail it through DHL mail service to Syria.

I informed your mother that the paperwork was on its way for her final approval and signatures and would arrive in Syria in seven to ten days. She was happy with that news and I continued to spend time with you daily until the paperwork arrived.

All options to smuggle you out illegally were now on hold. A week later we were going to meet at the church one last time before I left for America.

Finally the morning arrived when your mother and I were to meet at 10am in the church with the pastor. The paperwork from my attorney in America had not arrived as of this meeting, but I was planning to tell your mother and the pastor that it actually had.

The pastor began to write out a statement that he would present to the Archbishop summarizing our agreement. He asked if we were still on the same page as we had agreed to a week earlier. I immediately said that we were. I just wanted this thing to be over before your mother had a change of heart.

Then your mother began to speak. She said that, after a lot of thinking, she was backing off of our verbal agreement and now had different demands. She said that she was not agreeing to let me take you to America. She was now demanding, in addition to the large amount of cash we had agreed to, yet another amount of money to be paid on a monthly basis. She wanted the paperwork releasing her from liability in America and a signed agreement from me to give her a divorce.

"Let me understand this," I said to her. "You take my girls from a loving home in America, you kidnap them to Syria, you want a large sum of money for you, personally, you want a large amount of money on a monthly basis, a divorce, and no obligations in America? Is that right?"

"Yes," she said.

"And what do I get?" I asked.

"Well, you can come to Syria every year and see your girls," she said. "And by the way," she added, "If you don't agree to this, the only way you will see them again is in the church for two hours a week like the law says."

That was the lowest that I had seen your mother thus far.

"My girls are not pieces of real-estate," I told her, "and they are not going to be negotiated this way." I looked at the pastor as I was in shock at what had just taken place. "Do you hear what she is saying?" I asked him. "We both agreed to certain terms last week in your presence and now she has completely reneged on that agreement."

"Why the change of heart?" he asked your mother.

"These are my girls and they are better off staying here with me," she told him.

I was sick to my stomach and absolutely furious. I walked out and went back to Fairouzeh, where you both were at your uncle's house.

I picked you up and went back to Alfouhila. As soon as I got to Alfouhila, your mother called and said that she wanted me to bring you back home immediately. I told her that it was too dangerous then to take you back to Homs but, if she wanted, she could come to Alfouhila and pick you up herself.

She was very mean to me, especially now that she had not gotten what she wanted. I tried to shield you from what your mother was doing to me, but I'm sure the look on my face showed otherwise.

The next day your mother and her parents drove to Alfouhila and picked you up. I wanted so badly to tell you about how your mother was treating me, but I didn't want to break your heart. So I just gave you both a hug and kissed you goodbye before I left for America.

My flight was leaving in three days. With my vacation coming to a bitter end, I now had no options at all, since I would not be able to spend any alone time with you on that trip. My anger was turning into a blind rage and I found myself now thinking of very irrational and immoral thoughts. I went back to the house and just started crying. I began to throw things against the walls and to curse to the top of my lungs, screaming things I would never have said or thought of before. I was turning into someone I did not like. I sat there for hours plotting against your mother and her evil family. I thought of the worst things to do to them, but no matter what I could do, I was not prepared with a sound plan to get you out.

A couple of days later I went back to America and I would plan to see you on Christmas of 2011. I guess I was starting to accept the idea of going to Syria to see you both every six months, once on Christmas and once on your birthday in July.

Chapter 11

I began to call you on Saturday night, as requested, which made it Sunday morning in Syria, as opposed to Friday night like it was before, which was Saturday morning in Syria. I was more worried about you now than ever before, especially because you both were residing and going to school in the most dangerous city in Syria, the center of all the violence and demonstrations. By now innocent people were dying by the thousands.

I started to call on other days – like a Wednesday or a Friday – when we would hear of really bad violence, but I was not able to talk to you. I would call twenty or thirty times, but your grandparents would refuse to talk to me. It appeared to me that the responsibility that your mother had imposed on them was now getting to them and they were not happy. Your mother at this time had to make a choice since the company she was working for was relocating to Damascus due to the violence in Homs. Your mother decided to move to Damascus and leave you in the hands of your grandparents amidst the violence.

I was getting very upset that they would not pick up the phone when I called, and when they knew it was me, they would hang up. I would hear the voice of your grandmother as she pretended not to hear me and my heart would burn with anger to the point I would stay up all night thinking of paying them back evil for evil. That was not like me at all, but I could see that those people did not have an ounce of decency or humanity, keeping you from your father for their daughter's personal gain.

It went on for months. I would try to call every day and still they did not answer nor did they call me to at least give me some update about your well-being. Being so far away from you and not knowing what you were going through made me uneasy. And the lack of sleep for many nights was taking its toll on me, physically and mentally.

I remember one morning I woke up after an exhausting night of trying to call you and decided that, "enough is enough." Your mother had a cousin who lived close to us in California. He was someone who over the last few years had been a good friend to me. I always stayed in touch with him and he also kept in touch during the time that your mother was in Syria. I called him and told him about the situation in Syria and how I hadn't been able to talk to you for months.

I asked him to just listen to me for a few minutes and understand that what I was about to tell him had no bearing on our friendship. I began to tell him the story that he had heard before, but I wanted to remind him that I had exhausted every option for your mother to return to America with our children. I talked about the war in Syria and the danger my girls were in. "It is no longer about a marital dispute," I told him, "now it is about life and death.

I apologized to him in advance for what I was about to tell him and said that it was not intended towards him, but rather your mother's family for what they were doing to me and my children. I simply told him to imagine for a minute a scenario of the day after a desperate father commits an unthinkable act of violence toward a family, where he would possibly take the life of one of their children, and what people might say about him. I said some people would blame him for such an evil act, while others may hold him harmless for simply going insane and thus committing this act. But the end result would be devastating for everyone involved, including the children.

"So," I ended, "I am asking you, please talk to them and inform them that I am now in a state of desperation and will be held blameless for any action I will take against them. I am prepared to do whatever it takes. Please make sure that they have my girls in a safe place and that I am able to communicate with them."

He understood my situation and was very sympathetic. I did not wait for him to talk me through or out of whatever state of mind I was in. I simply hung up the phone.

I called Syria a couple of days later and finally got a chance to talk to you for a few minutes. I'm not sure what her cousin did or said to your mother and her family, but it seemed to work – for now.

I felt better once I talked with you. You sounded like you were doing well and that you were very smart in school and your sister was doing well, too. This was a turning point for me in the sense that I needed to get my life in order and build myself back up emotionally. But until I was able to bring you back to America, I didn't think my life could have any meaning. I was just waiting and counting the days until Christmas came and I would see you again.

I had spent a month and a half with you on that last trip and then I had gone back to work as usual. I had a plan for the next few months and that was to get a little more financially strong so that I could take some time off from work to see you again at Christmas of 2011, as I said I would do. I continued to talk to you every Saturday night. Most of the time it was at midnight or one in the morning my time, as your mother demanded.

Christmas Eve

Why are you lonely girl on Christmas Eve?
Is there no one there to hold you, on Christmas Eve?
Don't you cry now, wipe your tears now
Look above and you'll receive
Just remember Jesus loves you, please believe.
And why are you lonely boy on Christmas Eve?
Don't be sad now, just be glad now
Look above and you'll receive
He is watching and he loves you, please believe.
Your mind is full of wonder and your heart is full of joy.
So let's come together and have his spirit fill our souls
And there will never be, a tear drop from
your eyes or sadness on your face
What will be is laughter in the rain and footsteps in the snow.
We'll play together forever more, forever more.
And if ever you are sad, look above
And if ever you are lonely, look above
For this is Christmas Eve, and for that you shall receive
All his mercy and his love, please believe.

Chapter 12

My Third Trip to Syria

Things in Syria were bad and getting worse at this time. Thousands of people were dying, mostly in Homs, where you both lived and went to school. I was very worried about you and your sister. It seemed that there was nothing I could do. Your mother was not listening to me to move you to a safer place where you might live and go to school away from danger. I needed to go back to Syria and find a way to get you out.

Christmas 2011 came and I was not able to go to Syria on that date. I was unable to leave work as I had planned, but I did let you know that on the phone. I told you that I would be in Syria two weeks later. And so it was. I bought you and your sister the most popular toys and electronics, including your number one request, which was an IPhone for you and an IPad for your sister, along with many other things. I took a flight to Turkey and from there to Syria.

Before I left this time around, I wanted your mother to know that I was coming, so I tried to call you on Christmas Eve to wish you both a Merry Christmas, but your mother and your grandparents would not pick up the phone. I called every number and every cell number and still no one answered me. It was my birthday that night and I spent it at your Uncle Nick's house. It was the first Christmas that I would spend away from you and, needless to say, I was pretty devastated.

Christmas day I tried to call again. After many attempts, your mom finally answered. I said Merry Christmas and told her that I was coming to Syria in the next few days and hoped that I could spend some time with you girls without any problems. I said that, hopefully, we could come to some terms while I was there so that we could start to raise our girls the best we could under the circumstances. She was not happy that I was coming and said that I was wasting my time because I was only going to be able to see you for one hour per week.

"It's Christmas," I said. "Let's not argue."

She immediately handed you the phone. I talked to you both for a few minutes and told you that I was coming to see you very soon. You were very happy to hear that.

On January 7, 2012, I boarded a flight to Syria and I arrived on the 9th. My vacation was going to be short, just two weeks. Things in Syria were pretty ugly and every one was advising me not to go, that it was very dangerous. It's funny how people think when they are not in the hot seat. I understand that they were concerned about me, but I don't think that I was doing anything that any normal father wouldn't have done in my situation.

This trip was going to be different, I thought. I was more experienced now with flying to Syria and more comfortable getting around the city of Homs. It was a shame what was happening there. Just a few months previously, before the war broke out, I had considered moving there. It was only a thought that came to mind when my lawyer in Syria shocked me with the news that you would be in the custody of your mother until the age of fifteen, or even eighteen, if she were to raise an objection with the court.

I began to add up the years and found that by the time you and your sister were able to come back to America, I would be in my fifties. It meant that I would miss out on most of your childhood.

I drove myself to LAX Airport and then had your Uncle Diab, who lived close by, drop me off and take my car. I couldn't wait to see you. I had a long flight that would take me from LAX to Turkey and then to Syria. I had made arrangements with my cousin Zaid in Syria prior to leaving and told him to meet me at the airport in Damascus. My cousin has a taxi and lived in an adjacent village to where I would be staying, and I trusted him. I arrived in Damascus at 1:30 in the morning on the 9th. Already two days wasted in the air that I wouldn't spend with you.

It was dark and we were a little worried driving to Fairouzeh. We were told to be careful and to take side roads, due to militant groups possibly hijacking our car and then killing us. It was a common occurrence in the country.

I had rented the same house that I had on my last trip. We got there safely and without anything dramatic happening. It was then around five in the morning and it meant that I had to wake up the landlord and get the keys. The landlords were so sweet to me, an older couple who had come to like me and sort of understood that I came to Syria every six months to visit with my girls. They had built living quarters for their son on the second floor of their house, but he decided to make his home in America and, to my luck, the home was furnished with all the amenities one would need. The lady had it cleaned and ready for me.

"How long will you be staying this time?" she asked.

"I'm not sure, maybe a month," I said. I guess I was still untrusting at that point and did not want her to know that I would literally leave in three days if my plan worked this time around.

I took my bags and went up the unfinished concrete stairs and tried to settle in. I decided to make a trip by foot to the store that was near the house and fill the fridge with all your favorite things. As I was walking back to the house, there was a military vehicle loaded with soldiers. I was wearing a hooded jacket and sunglasses. As I passed them, they looked at me with suspicion. I guess it might have been the way I was dressed; it was not the normal local dress code. I walked upstairs and a few minutes later I heard a knock on the door.

I went to the door and asked who is was, but no one answered. *Strange,* I thought. *Perhaps it is my imagination or I'm just tired.* So I went back to sit down and again I heard the same knocking.

"Who is it?" I asked, going to the door again. And still no one answered. I got worried that it might be the military people following me, so I went to a side window that I could peak from and as I opened it, I heard a string of gunfire and realized that it was not a person knocking; it had been gunfire all along. I laughed a little to myself and went back to drinking my Arabic coffee that I was now addicted to. I began to watch the news to kill a couple of hours and then call your mother.

Around 9am I called her to say that I had arrived. She immediately said that she was busy. "Sorry," I said, "but I just want to know when I can see my girls."

"We'll see," she responded with her usual answer that seemed to always be on the tip of her tongue.

"I'm only here for two weeks so, please, let's not fight or argue," I said.

Again she said, "We'll see. I'm busy now," and hung up.

The gunfire was getting intense and must have been close by. My curiosity got the best of me. I went to the window and realized that there was a battle going on not far from the house. It was approximately a mile away, gauging the dust from demolished buildings. My mind began to think of where you might be at that moment.

I knew that you and your sister were in the heart of the bombing, just about ten miles from my present location. I wondered if you knew what to do in the event that, God forbid, your building was attacked. I knew you were smart, but I also knew that you were living with your elderly and disabled grandparents. How were they going to protect you like I would? The more I thought about that the more I was filled with anger and hatred towards them and your mother. How could they do this, how could they see what was going on in the country and not call me to just take you to America? Were these people sick in the head that they would risk the lives of my little girls for whatever personal or financial gain?

This is crazy. I am going to find a way to get my girls out on this trip, no matter the cost or risk, I thought. *No one is going to stand in my way this time. I am prepared to do just about anything, and I mean anything. Moral or not, right or wrong I don't care anymore. Enough is enough.*

I somehow fell asleep but woke up in a panic. I looked at my watch; it was 11am. I called your mother again. She said that it was test week at your school and, supposedly, your last day was Thursday. That would mean I would have to wait until then to see you, and even then she said, "We'll see."

I was getting very frustrated and angry. I was worried about you being in the city of Homs where, at that time, it was the very worst that it had been. People were being kidnapped and tortured. Others were being held for ransom and yet others were being chopped up into pieces and thrown in the middle of the street for people to see. You can imagine what was going on in my head, as every second felt like eternity to me. I tried to reason with your mother and inform her of the grave danger you were all in. But with a calm voice, she just brushed it off and said that it was not as bad as I was making it out to be. She said that she would call me and let me know when I could see you. That there would have to be some arrangements made first. I got off the phone and began to work on my plan.

I knew that the plan would have to involve some risk. I began to think of the steps your mother had taken to prevent me from simply taking you and just getting on a plane. Your mother had placed a restriction that prevented both of you girls from traveling outside of Syria. The corrupt Judge or Archbishop at the church gave her that order without hearing my side first. So now your names would prompt a red flag upon attempted exit to any bordering country, Lebanon, Turkey, Iraq or Jordan.

Also, even if there was a way to get out, there were necessary documents I would need to prove that I was your father. One of these documents was a family book that, in Syria, is essential for one to carry in order to get things done. Such as rationed items from the government or applying for aid or medical attention and, most importantly, travel documents, including passports, birth certificates and, especially, Exit Visas.

Your mother had forged my name and had possession of that book. But, most importantly, you and your sister were not with me. And that was going to be difficult for me, since she was only allowing me to see you under close supervision.

I decided to take a trip to see my sister in Alfouhila where I could think clearly. Alfouhila is where I was born and there I felt safer since it was about fifteen miles away from the problem areas. While I was there, I happened to run into a cousin who had become a high ranking officer in the Syrian army. Amir was an arrogant and handsome young man and very sarcastic. Somehow we got to talking about my visit and I thought he might be able to share with me some contacts that might help me.

Jokingly, he asked, "Are you thinking of flying out with your daughters? I may have to arrest my own cousin, and that is not going to be good with the family."

I laughed and said, "Oh, no, I was just needing some paperwork done and thought that you might know people that could make it easy for me."

"Consider your problem solved," he said, as he winked at me and smiled. "Will you have a drink with me later tonight?" he asked.

"Yes," I told him, "I will."

Vengeance is Mine, Says the Lord

Where will you hide from God's vengeance?
And what level of hell, if no repentance?
How deep are the wounds you have caused?
And how many praises for your name will be tossed?
Mercy, you had none. And none will be shown
Knock, and be denied, once he's on the throne
How low, below the valleys will you stray?
And what price to the devil will you pay?
Like a serpent, you deceive just to get your way
But little do you know, from a million miles away
He watches every step and every word you say
As such you'll be judged, come judgment day.

Chapter 13

I needed to get working on the documents quickly. I got on the phone to a girl I had the pleasure of meeting on my first trip to Syria. She was incredible at getting things done. She had gotten me a Syrian ID within one hour when it usually took two weeks. Amazing what you can do with the right contacts and a little bribery.

My friend's name was Leila. I explained to her my dilemma. She said that it was hard to do but she would try to help. She said that lately the office where she worked had come under many attacks and that they had only been opening about two hours a day.

It was now Tuesday and the following day we would meet at her house and she would take me to work with her and try to get all the documents I would need to travel.

"However," she said, "my boss calls me each morning before I go to work to assure me that things are safe. Hopefully they will be tomorrow. Meanwhile, I need you to have the following things prepared before I see you." She said I needed pictures of you and your sister and my passport.

I hung up with her and felt confident that things were looking up. I called my cousin Amir, and he asked me to meet him at his Uncle Jamal's house. I knocked on the door and was greeted by Amir and was introduced to his uncle, whom I have never met, and a strange fellow by the name of Nasser, who was Amir's driver and assistant.

As we began to talk, Amir's Uncle Jamal asked if I knew a girl in California by the name of Dalia who lived very close to us. I said I did.

"She is my sister-in-law, my wife's sister," he said.

My heart fell to my stomach. I looked at my cousin Amir and asked to have a word with him outside. I told Amir that the girl his uncle was referring to was my wife's best friend in America, that she knew all about my wife's intention to leave America and not come back with my children, and that she had agreed to keep it a secret. "So, I'm not sure we can trust your uncle at this point," I told Amir. "What if he speaks to his sister-in-law?"

Amir assured me that his uncle would take a bullet for him and that if I trusted him, I should trust his uncle, as well. We walked back inside.

Inside the house, Jamal offered to make us some Arabic coffee; it gave me a chance to reflect on Dalia's roll in all of this. She was one of the friends your mother was very close to. Dalia and her husband used to live close to us and they had a son who used to play with your sister. We trusted them and thought that they were good friends. They seemed genuine and we offered to help them many a time since they were not well off, financially. The thought that Dalia was in on the whole plan disappointed me, and the fact that her husband did not warn me was a bigger disappointment. I thought he was a friend. I found out that Dalia knew about your mother's plan long before she took you to Syria and she could have warned me, but she did not.

This whole nightmare could have been avoided had someone even given me a small hint. But I was used to people like that. Most of my life I had been surrounded by people that were simply just takers and who, for the most part, enjoyed seeing other people going through adversity.

"Now that you are relaxed, Cousin, tell me what you have in mind. And let me assure you that you can tell us everything, we are all on your side here," Amir said.

I began to tell them that I had been coming to Syria every six months, working on a plan to get my girls out. The last two visits had been unsuccessful, but I was able to achieve a few objectives each time and that now I was ready to move forward with my next plan.

"Here is what I need from you," I began. "It seems that my wife has placed a restriction on my two daughters at all borders of Syria. I need that lifted. Once lifted, I will need to find a way to get to my girls, take them by force, and drive them over the Lebanese border. Once there, the U.S. Embassy in Beirut will give us protection and help us with travel arrangements to America.

"I have done all my research," I said. "And I know what documents are necessary. I do have someone working on that and I will meet with them tomorrow. But there are two other things I need your help with. Let me explain more. I now have valid American passports for me and my girls. The State Department has voided the passports they initially came into Syria with.

"Their mother does not know that; she thinks that they are still valid. But this creates a problem. If we show the Syrian immigration these passports, they will inspect the pages and find that there are no entry stamps on them. And if we say that we lost the original passports, they would need a police report from the person who lost them – that would be their mother. Should Immigration have any contact with her regarding this, our plan is out the window.

"We need to find a way to deal with that. And the most important thing that needs to be done on the passports is they need to be stamped in Syria with an Exit Visa, otherwise, even if we flee to Lebanon, we would not be able to board any flight out without an exit stamp out of Syria and an entry stamp into Lebanon. This is according to the U.S. Embassy in Lebanon."

Amir's response was that he knew someone on the inside at the Immigration office and also his best friend was one of the captains at the Lebanese border, so with that said, he assured me, it would not be a problem. "Now," he said. "Let's talk about your girls."

The church we used to meet at had been bombed and was no longer occupied. So your mother had suggested that, if I wanted to see you, I would have to do it at her uncle's house in a village on the outskirts of Homs that your grandparents often went to on the weekends to avoid the constant gunfire where they were staying. I had agreed. And being that this was testing week, I wouldn't be able to see you until possibly Friday. That gave me about three days to get my plan together.

"I will see my girls this Friday or Saturday in a village called Alhafar," I said. "Do you know where that is?" I asked Amir.

"Yes," he replied. "That is the back way to Damascus and we use that highway often when we want to avoid going through Homs."

I said that after my visit there, I would gather as much information as I could on the location and the surroundings and we would meet there the following week.

"Meanwhile," Amir said, "let me write your daughters' names on a paper, and tomorrow I will check on their status with the immigration office."

The next morning I was to meet with my friend Leila. I woke up early, had a cup of coffee, and called my cousin Zaid to drive me to Fairouzeh so that I could get ready to meet with her. At 8am I called her and found her to be in a panic. She said that her boss had called her and told her that there was so much violence in Homs that day that she need not come in. I sighed with disappointment. I expressed to her that my time was very limited and I needed those documents. I was only a block from her house and she asked me to come over.

"I will go with you," she said, "but you need to hurry. We don't have much time. There is much bombings going on near the office."

In five minutes I was there at Leila's house. She called her father, who drove a taxi, and he met us outside in a matter of seconds. In the car there was me, Leila, her dad, and someone else I was not introduced to. On the way Leila asked if I had all she had asked for. I said yes. I motioned to the man in front with my eyes and she said that he was okay.

Leila's father was a rough-looking guy but had a reputation of knowing every nook and cranny of the streets of Homs. He immediately took charge and went the back way onto some dirt road and then onto the wrong way of an empty highway to Homs. The streets that were normally occupied by thousands of cars in heavy traffic were now wide open and vacant. There was nothing but military barricades, tanks and soldiers with machine guns. The sound of gunfire never stopped.

I was a little nervous but Leila said not to worry. "We are used to this," she said. "I go to work this way almost daily."

I shook my head. Each street corner was occupied by a military tank and soldiers. So we had to stop at each one for inspection. Upon inspection, all passengers had to hand their IDs to the soldier. As we started to get closer, the devastation of the buildings was indescribable. This was the street that only a few months ago had been beautiful and full of everyday people shopping and laughing and living a normal life.

Leila asked me to look in front of me and not to look conspicuous. The pavement was now covered with gun shells all the way to the office. A thought came to my mind: *there must be millions of shells on the pavement. How many of those possibly hit a child just by way of an accident?* I did not want to think about that too long. The streets reeked of garbage that had not been collected for months due to garbage collectors being afraid to take to the streets. The trash piles were about five feet high on every side of every street. The scene was like some third world country that had been devastated by some natural disaster.

Tears filled my eyes as I saw building after building half demolished by mortar fire. As we got close to the office, we had to maneuver through bricks and rocks and glass that had come from local storefronts that were now deserted. Finally, we got to the office and saw the chaos at the door. Hundreds of people were packed inside, trying to conduct their business. Leila's father dropped us off and left with the other gentleman. I was not prepared for this; in America we did not have to go through this. Everyone had a turn or took a number and waited to be seen.

Not here. Here, you needed to push your way through the crowd and, if you knew someone there, you had a chance, otherwise good luck.

Leila quickly grabbed my hand and began to shove me through this line of screaming people. She took the passport photos and began to make her rounds from office to office like an Olympic athlete. I was amazed by what I was seeing. She knew everyone in each office and bypassed the entire crowd in each one and got them to do what she wanted, with a wink and a smile, of course. As if to say, I will take care of you later.

This was a two-story building and she must have gone up and down those stairs several times to get the documents stamped by the appropriate officers. She was catching a sweat and I couldn't help but look at her and think, what an amazing girl.

"We only have one final signature," she said, "and then we are done."

I could not believe it. *God is with us*, I thought, *and is making things work out just right*. I had not even finished that thought when the building took a string of gunfire that made the chaotic situation ten times worse. People began to panic and huddle to the ground. The sound was deafening.

"What do we do?" I asked Leila.

She quickly took my hand again and pushed our way to the last office we needed signatures from. She saw a colleague standing next to the main officer who was to sign off our documents and called him by the name of Ammar. The officer told Ammar that she had gotten a warning from some militant group stating that the building would be hit in five minutes. The officer got on the speaker and asked everyone in the building to clear out.

The next couple of minutes were disastrous; people were shoving each other and, like a stampede, heading towards the only exit door. People were being trampled and screams were louder than bullets. Leila shouted for Ammar to come over and grab the document from her hand and have the officer sign it quickly. He did. The officer looked at him with disgust and grabbed the documents, almost shredding them, and signed faster than I have ever seen. She asked him to quickly stamp them and to move out in a hurry. I did not notice how many minutes had gone by, but we needed to hurry.

Leila asked Ammar if he had a car close by. "Yes, right outside the door," he said.

"Let's go. We are coming with you. This is a friend of mine from America," she said, introducing me to Ammar. We rushed towards the door that was by then almost clear. She again held my hand and we ran out the door.

We had not taken even a couple of steps towards the car before mortar fire began to rip the building to shreds. We were ducking and running. The sound of the gunfire was so intense I literally heard shells buzzing by our heads. Concrete dust from the walls filled the air. Finally, we were in the car and on the floor like sardines. Ammar was so nervous that he could barely put the keys in the ignition. Leila took charge again and yelled at him to get himself together and get us out of there. All we could do was brace ourselves as he tried to maneuver his way out of a tight alley. The gunfire was now more intense and we did not know what direction it was coming from.

He finally got onto a main street, only to find that the cars were now driving in reverse trying to get away from whatever they saw up ahead. So, quickly, he made his way into an even tighter ally to avoid colliding with anyone. As we entered the alley, we realized that we were in deep trouble as we were now faced with armed men wearing no military uniforms.

"Leila," I said, "we are in big trouble. These guys are part of a militant group that's against the government. If they find out I am an American, there is a big chance they will take me as a hostage."

She asked me to be calm and not to speak a word. My American accent was clearly evident when I spoke in Arabic.

Two armed men approached the car and asked Ammar to roll the window down. "What are you doing here?" the man asked Ammar. His automatic machine gun was halfway into the car.

"We were just taking care of some paperwork at city hall and now we are just trying to get home," Ammar replied, mumbling.

I looked over at Leila as she was holding all of my documents and I pulled them from her for safekeeping, as if that was the most important thing to do at that time. The man noticed me moving and immediately asked Ammar to back up the car into an adjacent alley.

My heart was racing a million miles an hour. I thought, *we are really in trouble now.*

Ammar obeyed the man and backed up the car into a tight space and continued to back up until he almost hit the building behind us. There we stood as gunfire in the background was almost unbearable. A minute later the man motioned for someone to notify another man inside the building. Possibly the man in charge, I thought. *Here is where the man will ask for my ID, find out that I'm an American and ask me to get out of the car.*

A man came out of the building and approached the car. He was not armed. He asked Ammar a few questions and was satisfied. He said in a few seconds he would give us the signal to leave. Those few seconds felt like eternity. A moment later the man said, "Okay, go on your way."

We just began to drive, not knowing where. "Just drive, Ammar," Leila kept saying.

The more we drove, the less gunfire we heard. After a while we ended up in the town where you and your sister lived and went to school. I asked Leila if she would come with me and there we could call and check up on her father.

"These streets are very familiar to me," I said. "Let me show you where my daughters are living." I took her and pointed to a third floor window where you and your sister lived. There appeared to be no one there. We continued to walk. I wanted to show her where you went to school. There were military personal on every corner, all the way to your school.

"Your wife must be crazy to want to keep her children here in this hell, when all she has to do is get on an airplane and go to America," Leila said.

I just shook my head and continued walking.

We finally reached the Christian school you both attended. It had a very big metal door surrounded by a ten-foot brick wall. I asked Leila if she thought it would be all right to knock on the door and see if I could see my girls.

"I'm not sure," she said, "but try it."

I knocked and soon a woman appeared and asked who I was. I said that my daughters went to the school and I wanted to check up on them. She opened the door and led us to the principal's office. A mean-looking woman came out and asked who I was. She immediately gave me a frightened look, as if she was prepared for this moment. She said that I was not able to see you or pick you up, only your mother and your grandparents had authorization to do so.

"No problem," I said. "I was just in the area and was hoping to say hi and make sure that they are safe, that's all."

Five minutes later your mother called my cell phone. I looked at Leila and we both knew that the principal had contacted her. I answered the phone. She asked where I was right then. "I am in Homs just taking care of some ID issues," I told her. "And, by the way," I said, "while I was in the area, I heard a lot of gunfire and shelling, so I thought I would check up on our girls and see if they were okay."

"Yes, I know," she said. "I heard you were there. But they will remain there until they finish their testing and then my parents will drive them to Alhafar for the weekend. You can see them then at my uncle's house. And we need to talk about some arrangements."

"Okay, see you then," I said.

Leila made a phone call to her dad and he met us to take us back to Fairouzeh. All I could do at that point was to wait in my apartment, watching news unfold about the possible warning attack on the Syrian international airport. *This is getting uglier by the day,* I thought. *What if it moves towards the border and hinders my plans. Best I can do now is wait 'til the weekend and continue to come up with a strategy to have my daughters spend at least one day with me with no supervision.*

Thursday evening I got a call from your mother saying that she was driving from Damascus to be with you and your sister since the next day, Friday, was a government day off. She also said that she may stay for the weekend. She asked me to meet a church pastor in that town who she knew well and to hand my passport over to him then meet her at her uncle's house where I could see you and your sister. I agreed and did just that.

I borrowed a family car and drove myself there. I knocked on the door of what seemed like a newly finished construction. It was wall-to-wall with your grandparents' old beat-up house that they used for the weekends. But this house was newly renovated and was really nice.

Your mother's uncle is big in build and stands over six and a half feet tall, by the way. Their whole family is tall.

The uncle, as well as his son and wife, were there to greet me. I walked in and a few minutes later they yelled for you from across the dividing wall and you and your sister came out to see me. It was so wonderful to see you both. As usual you did not come running to hug me; I always had to make the first move. But once you were comfortable, you showed me how much you had missed me.

My time there was to be short since we were somewhat imposing on these people who were now mediators between your mother and me. A few moments later, your mother showed up and I got up to shake her hand, nothing more. After the small chit chat, I began to reason and plead with them to please let my girls come home with me to America where it was safer. I mentioned to them that I had been in the area where they lived and went to school. "It is very dangerous for them to be there, especially when everyone in the neighborhood knows that they are Americans," I told them. "This is a cause for concern since the anti-government groups are targeting anyone who can draw attention to their cause."

I also went on to ask your mother's uncle a question. "You and your family lived in the heart of all the violence in Homs, and when you saw that your family was in danger, you moved them here to a safer place. Are not my kids entitled to the same thing from their dad? I am here and capable of securing their safety. Why are they any different than your kids or anyone else's kids who have left that area?"

I looked him dead in the eye and asked him, "What are you going to tell their mother to console her if, God forbid, something happens to my girls? 'My condolences?' What are you going to do or say to their father? 'The Lord giveth and the Lord taketh?' Is that what you might say to us? Do you want to take responsibility for what might happen and have it on your conscience?

"Let's all think rationally here. I am prepared to offer their mother anything she wishes and meet any demand you all want of me, just, please, let me take my girls to their home in America and take them away from all of this madness. What is it that you all want from me? Just ask."

Your mother's uncle jumped up and said, "We don't want anything from you. This matter is between you and your wife."

I looked at your mother and asked, "Just tell me what you want. You have witnesses here and whatever I agree to is binding. Just tell me."

She was looking at the floor and said, "My girls are not going anywhere with you. And after they finish with school, I was thinking of having them move to Damascus with me. Damascus is a very expensive place to live and my salary does not cut it. I need a minimum of 100,000 Liras per month for a nanny and to pay for their school and transportation and living expenses."

"Okay," I said, "is that all you need in order for them to move to a safer place? Consider it done."

She then went on to say that she would need more than that to have a home and things like we had in America so that they could live proudly. "I need more like 150,000 liras per month," she said.

At that time the highest paid state employee in the country only made 50,000 liras per month, but I said, "Okay, I agree, on one condition – that they do not go back to Homs from this day forward. No more school or anything else in Homs. Do you agree to that?"

She just got up and rushed towards the door. Then she turned around and said, "We don't agree to anything, it is me and my parents who will make decisions regarding my children," and then she slammed the door.

I just shook my head. Her uncle told me that any time on my trip I wanted to see you and your sister, just call him and come over. I was grateful. I can still see the look of disappointment on his face and the embarrassment that your mother caused him.

I began to see you for about an hour every other day at his house.

Through the Clouds

Don't you worry, and don't you fret
Soon will come a day, and you'll forget
Your troubles and worries will subside
Knowing that he is on your side
He is coming through the clouds
And we all will sing his name out loud
Hallelujah, the time is near
When the son on man will appear
He'll wipe the tears from your face
And comfort you in a warm embrace
Ninety nine angels, he promised to send
And a broken heart, he promised to mend
To the evil doers, in the day of wrath
He will deny them and hurdle their path
And to the believers whose lives were torn,
The one who wore the crown on thorn
Will raise them up and take them home.
Though they die, they are born.

Chapter 14

The road to the uncle's house was, for the most part, safe. There were about four Sunni Muslim towns along the way and two Alawite towns in between. I know that you normally would stop and ask me a question here, so I will try to clarify the conflict between the two religions. Syria consists of three major religious sects. The majority being Sunni Muslims which are about 70% of the population, the second being Alawites, which are about 20%, and the rest are a small group of Christians and others. This is part of the reason why there is a civil war in Syria. Syria's president is an Alawite, and Sunni Muslims do not like a minority group to hold power over the majority. They never have.

However, as long as I can remember, growing up in Syria this was never an issue. I went to school with students of both religions and we never even knew the difference. We were all friends and played and studied together. Now, with the so-called Arab spring, most Arab countries have taken to the streets for a change, although they, themselves, don't even know what that change will bring. So far, all Arab countries that have overthrown their current governments are suffering a great deal of chaos, destruction, fear and instability. And, most importantly, lack of peace. But this is a long subject and we will talk about it another time. For now, just know that I had to be extra careful as I passed through those towns, especially alone.

Being a Christian surely helps at times. Both sides, for the most part, like and get along well with Christians throughout Syria, and it seems these days we feel more protected since we are not in a position to take sides. We just mind our own business and kind of exist among the rest of the population.

There are many checkpoints that everyone must go through throughout the country, and one day I was stopped at a checkpoint where one of the military personal asked if I would remove the gold necklace he noticed on my neck. I did as he asked, and out came the cross I had been wearing for years. He just smiled at me and said, "You can go." He did not even ask for my ID, which is mandatory. I smiled, kissed my cross, and went on my way.

It was now Monday and your grandparents had taken you back to Homs against my wishes and this made me very angry. The situation there was horrifying as every bit of news showed the devastation and gory scenes of bloody bodies of men and children being dragged by men trying to dodge gunfire. I could not believe that your mother could be so stubborn and selfish to keep you there for even a second.

According to her, this week would be your last before you graduated the second grade. You would think that you were going after a master's degree and could not possibly miss this opportunity. I could do nothing but pray and wait. At that point, time was running out and I had only eight days left on my so-called vacation.

I called my cousin Amir to check on the status of his research with Immigration. He informed me that there did not seem to be a restriction on either you or your sister at that time. I was in shock. I couldn't believe it.

"There must be some kind of mistake," I said. "I know for a fact that there is, my attorney in Syria has already checked on this and confirmed that there definitely was and that was only six months ago."

Amir went on to tell me that he had a reliable source and that he had checked twice. He said that, possibly due to the current situation in Syria, it was possible the Syrian government removed all restrictions on foreign travelers. I could not believe it; I was incredibly happy and my heart was full of anxiety and joy. *This is going to be a piece of cake,* I thought.

Amir informed me that he would be in Alfouhila on Thursday and we would meet at his uncle's house once again for final details. I was on cloud nine and I could already see us on an airplane to America. I began to picture us back at home in America and starting our new life.

I wanted to celebrate this wonderful news. I had been invited to an *arak* brewing party and I had declined, but now I would do just that. *Arak* is an Arabic liquor that is normally brewed after a grape harvest in the summer, but a friend of mine knew how much I enjoyed the festivities of that event and had saved a batch for a special occasion. The man who holds such an event would invite his closest friends and relatives and have a large barbeque and they would have music and dancing and lots of drinking. I would drink like there was no tomorrow.

I was the happiest I had been in months. Everyone took notice but they did not know why. I must have also smoked a pack of cigarettes that night.

Tuesday morning I talked with your mother and was informed that you had completed your final exams and that Wednesday would be your last day at the school and, after that, your grandparents would again take you to Alhafar for the weekend.

On Wednesday afternoon I would drive to her uncle's house and see you there for a couple of hours. I called and confirmed. I arrived there at around six in the evening. While I was there, her uncle informed me that he was sorry, but this would be the last time I would be able to see you at his house because he and his family had been waiting for school to end so they could take a trip and see their son in Saudi Arabia.

He said that on Friday they would be in Homs to pick up some things from their house, so he made arrangements with your grandparents to receive me there at their house from then on. He said that he had arranged for that and I need not be uncomfortable since it was only for one hour. I thanked him for his hospitality and agreed to start seeing you at your grandparent's house. On the drive back to Alfouhila, where I was then staying regularly at my sister Mariam's house, I was thinking that God was making this so easy for me. Now that the uncle and his son were out of the picture, it was going to be much easier to get to you. After all, your grandparents were elderly and had no one but the ugly maid living with them, and maybe your mother, if she decided to drive from Damascus to see you for the day.

I could simply walk in with another guy, tie them all up, stick them in some dark closet with duct tape on their mouths and wait until we got into Lebanon before I would call and let someone know of their whereabouts, maybe. I would then take you and your sister and head to the border.

Of course, it would take a little bit more planning, but it was the first thought on my mind as it was getting dark. I had to focus on my driving through these little towns that either proudly had painted portraits of president Bashar on their concrete walls or they simply had nothing. Somehow I felt that if I were to break down in my car, I would want it to happen in an Alawite town. They were a little more understanding and closer to our way of life as Christians.

Thursday night I met with my cousin Amir at his uncle Jamal's house. Again it was me, Amir, his driver Nasser and Jamal. There was no time for small talk, so we just got to the business at hand. I began to tell them about the current events that had taken place since we last spoke. I said that this is an opportunity that could not be missed. Just as I began to speak, I got a phone call from your mother. I stepped outside for a minute and came back inside even more enthusiastic.

I told the guys that the plan had just gotten much easier; your mother was unable to drive to see you the next day due to some work issues.

"Gentlemen, this is my plan," I told them. "Tomorrow morning I will call my daughters' grandparents and ask to see them early that morning, saying that I only have a few days left on my vacation and that I can only see my girls that morning for an hour before I have to take care of some final shopping. Then I will call you and confirm that all is a go.

"I will take a taxi, but I will need someone to have a car ready for me waiting in Alhafar before I get there. He will park his car on the main highway. After I notice the car, he will receive a missed call from me indicating for him to follow us all the way to the house. There, he will park his car in a small alleyway next to the house after my cousin Zaid and I make our way in.

"I will have with me two bags of toys for my girls. One I will take with me and the other I will keep in the taxi. I will instruct my cousin to keep the taxi doors open and come inside with me; they know him, too, so it will not be uncomfortable for them. Once inside the house, I will ask to see my girls immediately.

"As usual I will show my girls what I brought for them. I will ask the grandmother to make us some coffee, which she usually takes care of herself and not the maid. At that point I will tell the girls that I have an even bigger surprise for them in the car. I will tell my cousin to keep the grandfather engaged in a conversation while I take the girls and go to the car to get the other bag.

"The alley next to their house, where the driver will be waiting for us, is merely ten feet away. We jump in and off we go. The whole process will, hopefully, take less than five minutes. If it should take longer than that, it means that there were more people there than were expected and we'll abort the plan for the day."

Immediately, Jamal volunteered to be the one who would be in the waiting car. I was incredibly grateful for that. He hardly knew me and he was willing to put himself in a very bad situation if things went wrong.

I continued telling them my plan. "Amir and Nasser will be in Damascus making the following arrangements: Amir, you will contact your captain friend at the border to make sure he is working that day and what his shift is. Second, you will arrange for a taxi driver who you trust and give him instructions of where to go and whom to see and what to do. As for the money for all involved, I will let you, Amir, handle it. Remember, there is no limit, just do what you need to do.

"The taxi driver will take us to the Lebanese border upon our arrival in Damascus. If you should experience any complications, you will let us know immediately, because if this is not one hundred percent safe for my girls, I will not go through with it, everyone must understand this point."

They all agreed.

As we sat there talking about the what ifs, Amir mentioned that if it was to fail, he would have no problem sending a police unit to the grandparents' house and forcefully taking you and your sister out and detaining whomever was present at that house indefinitely.

"No," I said, "I don't want my girls to go through something as traumatic as seeing their grandparents go through that or to be frightened to death by some strangers snatching them, either. We will stick to the plan for now."

That same night Amir called his contact on the border and confirmed that he was going to be there the next day starting at noon. His friend not only confirmed that he would be there but gave Amir instructions on what to do and whom he should see when our taxi driver arrived at the border. We had a final drink and I went back to my sister's house for the night.

Needless to say, I did not get much sleep that night. I played the plan in my head a thousand times. I was full of adrenalin and excitement. I was ready to face whatever consequences my actions would bring. At that time your mother was capable of pressing charges against me for attempted kidnapping and whatever else. I knew that she would not hesitate calling the police and having me arrested. The thought of being arrested and put in a Syrian prison did not sit well with me. Not because I was afraid, but because it would mean I couldn't be there for you and protect you if I were locked up.

In the back of my mind, I thought the worst case scenario would be that I would be locked up for a short time and then bribe my way out. I have heard of people getting out of murder cases for merely a few dollars thrown at some corrupt judge. And I was ready for that. But the one thing I could not bear thinking about was what the other men would also be faced with. They had nothing to gain and a lot to lose. They had families and children like mine. They were citizens of Syria and didn't have the choices like I had to leave. There was a lot at stake. I had to brush those thoughts to the side and focus on the day ahead. I began to pray.

The Good Wife

Like a sound red apple, and brilliant in decor
Clean on the surface, but rotten at the core.
The words that she speaks, as though of royal blood
But her spirit deep inside is tainted with mud.
How eloquent, the speeches she displays
And how quickly she recalls a biblical phrase
She may even charm you, with a wink and a smile
But the venom in her veins will sting for a while.
How clever are her ways, as she devises evil
No time to beware, and no time for retrieval.
Her life line derives from anger and strife,
Not much of a human, much less a wife.

Chapter 15

I awoke a little anxious. My sister asked if I could use some coffee while we had a chance to talk for a few minutes. "You look like you are up to something," she said. "What are you thinking about?"

"I just have some business I need to take care of today and I'm a little stressed," I told her.

She always had a positive thing to say, I loved that about her. Here was a woman who had suffered a great deal in her life and somehow she handled it with such patience and a great attitude. She had a daughter who was diagnosed with multiple sclerosis and hadn't been able to walk for over thirty years. She had two daughters married off to men in Argentina, a son that was in the United States with her husband, yet there she was, smiling and telling me that everything would be okay, just trust in God, that He knew what I was going through.

I couldn't help but think of a woman who had come to my work before I left America on this trip. This woman was about eighty years old and she had come in with her grandson with the help of an old cane. As she sat in my office, she noticed some pictures of you and your sister hung next to my desk. She asked about you and how old you were. Usually I would not open up a subject about my personal life, but she insisted on knowing more about you. I told her that you had been abducted by your mother and were now in Syria. I told her that I had been trying everything in my power to get you out, and that it was nearly impossible to do.

"Have you heard of the Patron Saint Jude?" she asked me. "He is the patron of impossible things. He is the one to pray to when you have exhausted all your options." She reached into her purse and took out a prayer card with his picture on it and gave it to me. "If you pray that prayer on the card," she continued, "he will help you with your dilemma."

I respectfully took it, thinking why not? I remember after she left, I said the prayer and asked Saint Jude to help me.

On Friday morning, as planned, I called your grandparents and asked if I could come over to see you that morning. I apologized for calling on such short notice, but that I did not have any other time to see you that weekend. Your grandmother said okay.

I then called my cousin Zaid and asked if he would drive me to Alhafar and bring me back. He said that he would be there in thirty minutes. I contacted Jamal and gave him the green light to drive to the spot on the highway we had talked about and asked him to call the others and inform them that we were in motion. I had prepared one piece of luggage for him to bring along that had all of my personal belongings in it.

I kissed my sister goodbye and gave her a big hug as that might be the last time I would see her until she found her way to America. She said that she was preparing my favorite dinner that night and that I shouldn't be late. I just smiled and agreed.

I jumped into the taxi and asked Zaid to stop by a pastry shop to take something for the grandparents and to pick up some smokes. Yes, I began to smoke regularly while I was in Syria. I couldn't help it with so much going on.

The drive was uneventful for the most part. We talked about Zaid's family, his children and how big they had grown. He asked how things were going with me and your mother. I did not want to talk about that much, but I asked if he could do me a favor when we got to your grandparent's house and keep your grandfather company while I spent some time with you and your sister. He said no problem.

I was focusing on the road, looking to see Jamal's car. The drive from Alfouhila to Alhafar was about twenty minutes, which meant that Jamal had already arrived by then. I had already smoked three cigarettes, I noticed, and promised myself that I would quit completely once we were in America.

I spotted Jamal's car parked on the side of the highway and called his number. I kept looking in the rearview mirror until he pulled up and began to follow us. The plan was going great so far. I was confident. I did not want my cousin Zaid to know anything about what was happening so as not to involve him with any wrongdoing. He was simply doing his job as a taxi driver.

As we approached the house, I noticed that Jamal was close behind us, about a hundred feet or so. We parked the car in front of the house and that was when Jamal disappeared from sight. *He knows what to do now*, I thought.

We got out of the car and I took one bag with me and left the other in the back seat. Zaid locked the car, and I asked him if he would please just keep it unlocked. He did not understand why. I told him I wanted to surprise my girls with the other bag later and that I might come back out and get it for them. He looked puzzled but obliged.

The front door of the old house was a two-sided metal door. I knocked and was greeted by the maid. Your grandmother was standing behind her and motioned for us to come in. The maid then went back to her quarters and your grandmother led us to the salon where guests usually were greeted. We walked inside and found only your grandfather smoking, as usual. He did not seem happy to see me but immediately began to converse with Zaid about the last time they had seen each other.

I asked about you and your sister. Your grandmother said that you had just woken up and that you were still in pajamas. I asked if she would let you know that I was there. She went to get you while I scoped out the surroundings.

My heart was beating so fast I could barely sit still. A minute later you and your sister walked in, wearing your pajamas and your new boots I had bought for you in America. You two looked so silly but completely adorable.

Your grandfather asked my cousin to join him in another room for a smoke. Zaid stood and followed him out the door to an adjacent room. That left only your grandmother. I asked if she would mind making us some coffee, and she quickly disappeared out of sight into the kitchen, which was about thirty feet away at the end of the house. I could not believe it. *This is too easy*, I thought.

As soon as she left, I grabbed both of your hands and took off towards the main door. I told you that I had a big surprise for you outside in the car. I flung the metal door open and it squeaked so loud I thought for sure someone would hear it and, in the rush, my shirt got stuck in the hinge and slowed me down for what seemed forever. A second later I was outside. With my hands tightly wrapped around both of you, I shoved you towards the alley next to the house which was only about ten feet away. My heart came to a sudden stop when I saw no one there waiting for us. I looked around the house but no one was there. I panicked; I could not understand where Jamal was. I thought that something had gone terribly wrong.

I went back and got the other bag from the car and made my way back to the house. As I was coming in, your grandmother was on her way back to the salon. She noticed that I was outside. I quickly said that I had forgotten a bag in the car and I was just getting it. She gave me a look that said I was not telling the truth. She looked frightened.

She immediately called for the maid to take care of the coffee as she followed us back into the salon. She did not want to sit down. She somehow knew that something was up but could not figure it out. Her speech was now shaky and slurry. And in that moment of panic, my mouth was dry. I quickly began to cough like I was almost choking and asked if she would please get me some water. She stopped for a second like she was confused but made her way towards the kitchen again. I grabbed your hands again and rushed towards the door without incident this time.

I knew where I had to go. I ran to the alleyway thinking, please be there, please be there. Sure enough, Jamal was there this time. I opened the back door and shoved you and your sister inside. I sat next to you and yelled, "Go, go, go."

No time to ask Jamal about what had happened. I just kept looking back to see if anyone was following us as Jamal made his way to the main highway towards Damascus. Inside the car, you and your sister were both asking me, "Where are we going, Daddy? We are not even dressed, we are still in pajamas."

"This is a surprise and we are going to Disneyland," I told you, "but first we are going to stop by a shopping mall and get some new clothes for all of us. Isn't that right Uncle Jamal?" Uncle Jamal smiled and agreed. All I could do at that point was smile.

I was not worried about anything. All I wanted to do was get to our destination in Damascus, get into the designated taxi, and drive to the border. I asked Jamal to make a phone call to Amir to confirm and ask for the location where we were to meet. Jamal was told to go to the transportation depot in Damascus where there were taxis, buses, and many people gathering there, so we would not be easily detected.

A taxi driver would be waiting there for us who would have all the instructions. I was now very confident, but one thing remained that I needed to do. I must call my cousin Zaid and let him know what had just taken place. For all I knew, he was being questioned about our disappearance.

I called his cell number, and he answered the first ring. "Listen, cousin," I told him. "I have the girls, and I am on my way back to town. Sorry I did not tell you, but I just want to spend a couple days with my daughters alone before I go back to America. Tell their grandparents that I will return them on Sunday and not to worry." I hung up before he could get a word in and I shut off my phone. I told Jamal to pay attention to incoming calls because my phone was shut off.

All the way to Damascus we sang tunes that you and your sister had learned in school and, I must say, I was very impressed with your Arabic skills; you almost spoke better than Daddy.

With minor traffic along the way, the trip took us about an hour and a half. Normally it would take over two hours. Jamal made a call to Nasser and we met at the depot. We noticed Nasser waiting on the sidewalk. We illegally parked and Jamal stepped out to speak with him. I heard a loud commotion between them as both of them seemed to be arguing. I stepped out of the car and found that the taxi driver Amir had designated to take us to the border had changed his mind at the last minute. He claimed that it was too dangerous to drive on that highway at that time and that there was gunfire along the border.

We were all looking at each other, not knowing what to do next. I guess we had not planned for this. I asked Nasser to call Amir and get his opinion. After a few minutes, Nasser hailed a taxi. I asked what he was doing; he said that he knew someone who would take us. An old beat up taxi the size of a fridge pulled up with an elderly scruffy man and a young boy in the front seat. Nasser told me that the old man was someone he knew and that he agreed to take us to the border. "I will take care of him later," Nasser went on to add, "So don't worry about paying him. I also gave him the names of the men he will see once you get to the border."

I took Nasser to the side and whispered, "This guy does not look Christian."

"No, he is not," Nasser replied. "But it will be okay, he is harmless."

I reluctantly agreed because we had no other choice at that point. We were already committed and must leave as soon as possible before a police report was issued. Normally a police report cannot be issued for civil cases until after twenty-four hours have passed.

We got into the small taxi that could barely fit two adults. It had no seat belts to speak of. It was one of those things where you ride at your own risk. It had been blackened with dark curtains on all the back windows.

There were hundreds of taxis, and for us to be stopped by police was unlikely. Besides, police at that time were so busy with the war going on they never bothered to investigate small civil cases. I was very confident we were going to make it. The drive, according to the taxi driver and his sidekick, who turned out to be his son, was less than an hour, God willing. I asked the driver to stop by a store to pick up some snacks and something to drink for you and your sister.

Once we got on the freeway, I noticed a sign up above the road that read, "Lebanon," with a couple of arrows leading the way. My mind was now at ease. We did not talk much on the way. You and your sister were playing with my personal phone from America and it had some games on it that kept you occupied for the most part.

I was paying attention to the road and began a journey in my head of what I would do first as I made my way to America. How many people would be there at the airport waiting for us and welcoming my daughters back home? That gave me a smile. I noticed the landmarks on the way and the terrain. It was mountainous and we could see the snow-covered caps of the Lebanese mountains. I noticed a building to the side that seemed like a factory and it had the same name as yours.

This must be a sign from God, I thought, and I began to take photos of it and of different scenes. The driver did not like that and asked me to put the camera away. He said that they might think that I was some spy if I were to get searched. I quickly deleted the picture and put the camera away. I thanked him for taking the risk to drive us, but he dismissed my gesture and just kept driving.

From a distance on the straight highway, I could see several military vehicles on either side of the highway and possibly thirty to forty soldiers gathered around. There were no tanks that I could see, other than atop the hillsides we had been passing. On both sides of the highway was a desert scene with tall grass that was almost uniform like grain fields. It was still light out and we noticed that, in addition to the soldiers on the side of the road, there were others scattered in the tall grass, possibly chasing or searching for someone.

The driver slowed down as we approached the military vehicles at a checkpoint. This was not part of the plan. I was more worried about the fact that our driver and his son were Sunni Muslims and that, as I had learned, most of the checkpoints were manned by Alawite personnel. *I just hope nothing happens,* I thought.

About thirty feet away from a complete stop, shots rang out in the fields next to us. I shielded both of you and pushed you to the floor of the taxi. The driver was yelling a prayer for God to help us. He made it to the checkpoint. I was terrified. I did not know what to do or what I had possibly gotten us into. The driver rolled his window down and was approached by a military man with an automatic machine gun slung over his shoulder who looked in the car.

"Where are you going?" he demanded. He asked for Syrian licenses for the three of us. We were the only car for miles on that stretch of highway. He inspected our IDs and asked who the little girls were.

The driver informed him that I was their father and that I was taking them to see an uncle in Lebanon and also to do some sightseeing. The man looked at me as if to size me up, looking closely at my Syrian photo ID.

He asked the driver to open the trunk. I was worried about what he might find; I began to take mental inventory of my personal belongings and wondered if he might help himself to anything. He asked the driver to get out. I was panicking, I did not know what he had noticed, if anything, but a moment later the trunk was closed and we were on our way.

The border was now merely ten miles away but seemed like a thousand. We got to the part of the border that we will, for now, call the pre-border. It was where taxi drivers or travelers stopped and got documents stamped, as well as applied for Exit Visas.

We needed that done, as I mentioned before. Without those stamps, it was useless to go across the border. We would just be changing locations, which did not seem like a bad idea. *Maybe we can just live in Lebanon if all else fails,* I thought. I would not be able to go back to Syria because I would be facing jail time for kidnapping and I would not be able to go to America without an Exit Visa out of Syria.

The driver called Nasser to check if he was in the right place. "Yes," he was told, and he was reminded to ask for a certain individual. The driver parked his car lopsided along with the rest of the so-called drivers stopped at the checkpoint.

The driver exited the car and went into a small building at the side of the road. Moments passed and finally he came out. I did not like the look on his face. He informed me that the man we were asking for was not on shift and the man currently on duty was not able to help us due to the fact we did not have adequate paperwork.

I began to panic. "Listen," I said. "You need to go back inside and give that guy anything he wants. Just get it done. We have no choice here, we are not going back." I handed him $500. "This will do the trick," I told him. "Just be careful how you deal with it."

He listened and went back inside. Five minutes later he came out again, not looking like he had accomplished anything. He said that the money was not enough, the guy was asking for more.

"How much more?" I asked. He did not respond. A sour feeling came over me and thought, "Here we go again, yet another guy trying to milk more money and take advantage of our desperate situation."

Without going into the pantyhose stash wrapped around my stomach, I reached into my pocket and cleaned out whatever I had, which was another $200. I handed it to the driver and told him, "This is it. I'm not giving him anymore."

He took the money and disappeared back into the building. A few more minutes passed. When he came back out, he seemed to have a little bit more step. He entered the taxi and said, *"Ya Raab,"* which meant we were good to go. I was incredibly excited and thanked God.

I hugged you both and off to the border we continued to drive. At that point the border, where we would meet with my cousin's contact, was a mere mile away. After that, we were free.

My heart was pounding with anticipation, and I forced my dry lips to smile a little. I used to calculate your arrival in America by each long year, and now I was counting the minutes. Based on my mental calculations, we would be at the border in a couple of minutes and at the checkpoint in maybe another five minutes. *Okay, make it ten, just in case there is a jam*, I told myself. *And another ten minutes for the Lebanese side to verify documents, so all in all about thirty minutes to freedom.* What could go wrong?

That made me so relaxed. *I am finally going to come through on my promise to take you and your sister to Disneyland the minute we make it to California. We will stay in a large suite at Disneyland hotel and relax for a couple of days before I tell everyone the news. We will plan a party and invite everyone over for a large celebration with piñatas and balloons and clowns.* So many pleasant thoughts were running through my head. I could not stop thanking God for making this so easy.

I asked for the driver's name so I could put it in my journal when I got the time to write a story about my journey to bring you both home. *We can even have someone make a movie about this,* I thought.

I could see from the short distance that we are approaching the border. There were offices or checkpoints on both sides of the now two-lane highway. Concrete slabs divided the highway leading to them. There was no way to make a U-turn, but who needed one? The driver came to a slow stop, rolling just enough to locate a place to park the vehicle while he went inside the building on the left to get final approval from our source. Our driver asked me for the passports.

This is in the bag, so no need to panic now, I thought. *Our driver knows what to do and in a few minutes he will come out with a smile.*

As he closed the door of what I will call my favorite taxi from now on, I felt the need to really pray. I asked you and your sister to hold hands and repeat after me. "Thank you, Lord, for being with us and keeping us safe, and please, Lord, be with us, all the way to America, in Jesus name, amen." From my vantage point in the taxi, I could see the distance of the very last office or checkpoint was less than fifty feet away. On the right side, it reminded me of a toll road window like we have in America, but with the size of a small office. It was hard to believe that in a few minutes I would be able to look back behind my shoulder and say, "We made it." I looked at my watch; it was 4:05 and our driver had been gone for about five minutes. I did not want to start a new conversation with his son, nor did I really want to talk with you or your sister. I was in a different world and I just wanted to focus my thoughts on what might be going on with our driver. I did not want a single thought of doubt to occupy my mind.

The wind was picking up, I noticed, and I looked at you and your sister in your pajamas. It was getting cold and I was not prepared for that. We had not had time to stop and get some new clothes, but that was the least of my worries. Certainly, they would have a mall in Lebanon where I could simply walk into a children's boutique and have some young, beautiful Lebanese girl play dress-up with you and your sister as I sat and watched her come up with twenty outfits to take with us to America.

Ahmad, our taxi driver, opened the car door, startling me and disrupting my thoughts. Before I could get a word in, he said that the Captain would like to see me.

"Why? Is everything okay?" I asked with panic in my voice.

I did not know what to think at that point. So many things were going on in my head that I was almost feeling dizzy. I wanted to go, but I was almost afraid of what I might hear. If everything was all right, what did he want to see me for? After all, he knew my situation quite well. He knew that we had some issues, but that was why Amir chose him over anyone else.

"Does he want to see my girls?" I asked.

"No, he just wants to meet you in person," Ahmad said.

I was more confused than before. Do I just leave my girls with these strangers while I go inside? I looked at you and your sister as you sat in the back of that taxi, looking back at me for some answers or comfort.

How long can this take? I thought. *Maybe he just wants to shake my hand before I leave Syria and ask me to send his regards to my cousin Amir.* Yes, that could be it. After all, it would not be nice of me to just drive off without at least shaking the hand of the man who made this all possible, would it? Besides, what could these men really do? It was a one-way path to the Lebanese border and they would need documents stamped before the last checkpoint let them pass.

"Okay, let's go," I said. I bent down and whispered in your ear that I was only going to go inside for five minutes to get us something to drink and sign some papers. "You and your sister are going to wait for Daddy in here 'til I get back," I told you. "I need you to be strong for Daddy and keep an eye on your sister, okay, Baba?"

Not that a confirmation was necessary, but it would have been nice. You simply just looked at me with those scared eyes as if to say, "Hurry up, Daddy, let's just go home."

I took the passports from Ahmad and asked him to keep an eye on you and your sister. But he told me that he was coming with me and that his son would keep watch. That made me more comfortable. The building reminded me of a DMV office in the States. It started with a line of windows, and behind each one stood a uniformed officer specializing in whatever field. We passed all of them as Ahmad led the way to the office located way at the end of the building at a point that I could no longer see the outside.

We came to the glass door of an office that was occupied by three desks and three men. I wondered which one of these men was the man I was to see. I was hoping that it was going to be the one with the big oak desk and not the other ones made of rusted metal.

We were motioned to walk in. Ahmad immediately went over to the man with the oak desk and it made me more confident that we were speaking with the one who had authority.

The man stood up to greet me and I shook his hand with a smile that could be detected as a nervous one. "Relax my friend, you've made it," he said. He introduced himself as Aziz.

"My cousin Amir sends his regards. He thinks highly of you," I told him.

"Yes, Amir is a good friend," he said. "How are your daughters doing?"

"They are doing well, I just can't wait to get back home," I replied.

He began to talk of a friend he had in California and I had to act interested. The phone on his desk started ringing and as he went to pick it up, the man at one of the metal desks quickly transferred the call to his desk and told Aziz that he had it. Aziz and I continued talking about the friend in California and whereabouts he lived.

The man on the right was now asking for our passports while he was on the phone. I did not think much of it, so I handed them to him. He was speaking with someone on the other end of the line who, it appeared, was asking him to spell the names as they appeared on the passports. He began to sound off each letter in English and then in Arabic. I was not easy about what was happening, but I thought we were in good hands, so no need to panic.

"Are you sure?" the man said as he hung up the phone. He quickly walked over to the third desk there and asked the man to check on our passports. Before Aziz could get a grip on what was going on, the third man had already punched your names into the computer.

"*Seedi*, (Sir) you need to look at this." He was pointing to what appeared to be a flashing red line with your name and your sister's, as well.

"My friend, there appears to be a problem with your children's documents," Aziz said.

Acting confused, I asked, "What kind of problem?"

"It seems that your daughters have a restriction on any type of travel and this type of restriction cannot be lifted except by their mother or a judge," he said.

I could not feel my body at that point. My body must have gone into shock and my knees were beginning to almost buckle like I was about to fall flat on my face. My lips went dry and my words began to slur, every word after that. I must have looked like I had just seen a ghost. Aziz asked me to sit down. A million thoughts went through my mind, but all I wanted to do was to go back and check up on you and your sister.

What is this guy talking about? I thought. *Of course they have a restriction, that is why we are here talking to you,* I thought in my head. Was this some kind of a joke? Would my own cousin put me through this, knowing this might happen? Did he not understand when I told him how important it was for this to be one hundred percent safe for me and my children? This could not be happening. We were so close. I had to do *something.*

Aziz went to sit down at his desk and I felt the need to speak to him alone, but that was not going to be easy to do. I stood and leaned down, whispering to him, saying, "Please, see what you can do. Amir sent me here to see you, personally. He said that you would be able to help me. Please, is there anything you can do? I cannot go back. I need to take my daughters and go back to America."

Aziz whispered back, saying, "Your cousin Amir did not give me the correct spelling of your daughters' names when we last spoke. Your daughters have a middle name that he did not mention, so it appeared to me that there was no restriction on such names at that time."

Aziz no longer had the smile that he had earlier. He looked like he was about to say something I would not like to hear. But he took a deep breath, and in a frustrated and disappointed tone of voice, he said," You need to take your girls and go back to Damascus. Maybe you can work something out with your wife and try again another time."

I was not convinced. I tried to pump up his ego. "Mr. Aziz," I begged, "you are all I have right now. If anyone is going to help me, it is you," and I reached into my pocket and pulled out a wad of whatever money I had and discretely shoved it next to his smoking ashtray. That would prove to be a big mistake.

Aziz took the money and got up from his chair, laughing as he called on his assistants to look at the money I gave him. "Look at what this man just tried to do," he said in a sarcastic tone. Then he looked at me with a fading smile that turned into a very serious look. "Let me ask you something, my friend. Do you walk up to a policeman in America and hand him money to take care of business for you? Or go to a military officer and entice him with a bribe and not face an arrest or jail time? I am very much aware of your laws in America," he added.

I was now a nervous wreck. I quickly said that I was very sorry and that I did not mean any disrespect by it. "It was merely a gift for you and the guys to grab some lunch for going through all this trouble, that's all," I told him. Granted, the money was enough to feed them lunch for a month, but it was all I could come up with at that time.

Aziz walked closer to me, almost face to face, and asked, "Do you think that you Americans can come here and just waive a few dollars around and get what you want, is that it?"

"No sir," I answered, "not at all. Please forgive me. I can see that I have upset you and I can assure you that my intentions were not to do that." I must have looked so small to everyone there watching. It felt like I was being reprimanded like a criminal. *What have you done?* I blamed myself. *You have put yourself in danger and worse, you have put your daughters in danger.* I kept thinking to myself, *I need to get out of this somehow.*

This Aziz was no longer the friendly source Amir had told me about. Was he possibly just acting that way to show his assistants that he had no idea about any of our plans? Maybe he was sending me a hidden message, but I was too tired to figure out riddles at that point. I was very scared and concerned about the outcome of the situation I had gotten myself into.

This must be the moment I have so many times thought could happen, I thought. *This is when I will be sent to jail and have to deal with Syrian prisons. What will happen to my girls? Who is going to take them back to their mother? And what are they going to feel as their father is being hauled away like a criminal right in front of their eyes?* These awful thoughts were debilitating.

Ahmad, seeing me struggle, stepped forward and, in the simple, Syrian traditional words one would use to sway another, asked Aziz to forgive my mistake. "Sir," he said, "He did not mean anything by it. He has been away from Syria for most of his life. Please, forgive him, and we can just go on our way". That seemed to work, as Aziz handed the money back with disgust and told Ahmad to take me and go straight back to Damascus.

I wanted to shake Aziz's hand and apologize once again, but I just hung my head low on my way out the door. I could not wait to get to the car to check up on you and your sister, but I was still thinking of a way out of going back to Damascus.

As we approached the exit door, I noticed that the taxi was not where we had left it. As a matter of fact, it was nowhere in sight. My heart stopped for a second and a barrage of bad thoughts took over my mind. I was panicking but did not want to show Ahmad that I did not trust him.

Suddenly, a van moved on toward the border, and I saw our small taxi hidden behind it. I rushed over and got inside. I gave you both a big hug and a kiss.

"Are we going now, Daddy?" you asked.

"Yes, sweetheart, we are."

Getting into the taxi was hard to bear. I felt every type of hurt, resentment, anger, frustration and, worst of all, and for the first time, I felt like I had failed my daughters. Guilt and disappointment took a hold on my heart and all I could do was just hold you both in my arms and hope that Aziz would just come running outside and tell me that there had been a mistake. I hoped that God would interfere at the last second and miraculously find us a way out. *We are so close*, I thought. *I can throw a stone farther past this wicked border.*

"What do you want to do now?" Ahmad asked.

Needless to say, I was speechless and asked him to please give me a moment to think. I began to replay the events in my head and pinpoint where we went wrong. Not that it was going to make any difference, but it seemed like the thing to do since I did not have a plan B at that time. It was going to be dark soon, I thought. "We need to get back to Damascus," I instructed Ahmad.

Ahmad started the car and straightened it out facing the Lebanese border and began to move forward to the checkpoint. It was the only way we could make a U-turn. *What if they don't even ask any questions?* I thought. *Maybe they will just overlook all protocol and simply tell us to keep going. Yes, that could happen, I have heard of things like that.*

We were now at the checkpoint and were met by two military men with machine guns. One man went to Ahmad's window while the other scoped our car and who was in it. I could hear the man questioning Ahmad about where we were headed and I couldn't help noticing that we were now the closest we had ever been to freedom. If only someone would come and attack these borders, I dreamed, and these men would have to leave us and go fight the enemy. We would then just drive away and be in Lebanon before anyone knew what happened.

My daydream was quickly interrupted by a man who looked familiar running towards our car. When he got there I realized that it was the man in Aziz's office, the one who had ruined everything for us. *What the hell does he want now?* I thought.

He was almost panting like a dog as he was trying to explain our situation to the military men. Whatever he told them was enough for them to immediately draw their weapons and asked us all to get out of the car. The man on the right ordered Ahmad's son to get out. I did not need any instructions; I opened the door and grabbed you and your sister's hands and stood next to the car until we could figure out what was going on.

Ahmad and his son were taken to the side by one man and you, your sister, and I were asked to wait next to the wall. It was now very cold and windy. I tried as much as I could to shield you both with my body, as you were still in your pajamas and had no jackets. I did not know what was about to happen, but the thought of your mother came to my mind. I knew that by then your mother would have called the police and filed a report.

But I also knew that, with the chaos of what was happening in the country, they would not consider this to be top priority. Not unless she called on her aunt, the Congresswoman. *I bet she did,* I thought to myself. *I bet she called her aunt and then her aunt called some high military officer who owed her a favor and he tracked us down to the border.* But now what? What can they do to us now? Was your mother or the evil aunt capable of doing something foolish?

My blood was boiling with anger. *If only I had a gun,* I thought. *I would not hesitate for a minute taking out all these men at once and then get in this taxi and drive us the hell out of here.*

The man on the right noticed that we were cold and told me to bring you and your sister into his office. At least I thought it was an office. It turned out to be just a concrete floor with a bus stop-like bench to the side, shielded by four walls to protect us from the wind. It concerned me, being there. The man had the demeanor of an interrogator. After all, for the last year or so, after you were taken to Syria, all I had seen on TV was investigative shows dealing with criminals and murderers and interrogations. I knew his type. First they act concerned for you and your kids, and then they begin the questioning.

I was ready, but reality set in when he began to question my motives for taking you out of the country. I was prepared with an answer for just such an occasion, which was that I was simply taking my daughters to Lebanon for a little vacation to see the sights and do some shopping for the weekend and then coming back. But he did not look like he was going to buy it. So I decided to tell him the truth. I told him that your mother had brought you to Syria on an alleged two months' vacation and decided to keep you indefinitely. And now I was here to take you back to your home in America.

I explained to him that I was your father and that I had the right to be with you and to travel with you and could not understand why I was being treated like a criminal. I lied and said that I had no idea that my wife had placed a restriction on you traveling to Lebanon, but when I got to Damascus, I would have my lawyer look into it and find out what was going on.

He seemed to sympathize with me and called on his partner to come over. The two men whispered to each other then they both went outside to talk with Ahmad. They asked me to follow them. With authority, the one man looked into Ahmad's eyes and in a strong and stern tone of voice said, "You will take this man and his children back to Damascus this minute. This minute, do you understand?"

Ahmad nodded his head, agreeing to the order.

We got into the taxi again and, with one military man on either side of our car, they walked alongside, passing the border by about twenty feet to the end of the concrete barricade dividers so that we could make a U-turn and head back towards Damascus.

The Pre border to Lebanon from our Taxi

The Syrian and Lebanese border

The silence in the taxi was deafening. I could hear the pounding of my heart as if it were about to burst out of my shirt. Despair was setting in, and as much as I tried to force a smile from my lips to at least ease your mind and give you both some comfort, I could not. I could see your lips moving as you talked to me, but it was nothing more than a muffled sound against the overwhelming thoughts playing in my head.

I was trying hard to see some good out of this. I always had a belief or superstition that things happen for a reason. I recalled an old Muslim quote that my dad used to tell me whenever something did not go my way. He would say, "*La takrahu shayan, la allahu khayran lakom*" meaning, Do not hate anything, for it may be a blessing to you.

Maybe God just wants to keep us from harm? Maybe if we had continued on our way to Lebanon, something bad would have happened and God is protecting us by not letting us go through with this plan, I thought.

I wanted to call my cousin Amir and tell him a few choice words for making such a rookie mistake, but he had risked his job and reputation to help me after all, so I would just take this as a learning experience and hope to prevent such a mistake on my next attempt.

I really did not know what to talk to you and your sister about. I couldn't look you in the eye and tell you what I was feeling about your mother and her family at the time. I did manage after a while to tell you that today was not the right time to go to Disneyland. That the roads were closed and we would have to try another day. I was amazed at your understanding.

You either felt my pain or it was evident on my face. You held my hand tighter and said, "It's okay, Baba, we will just go another time when we are better dressed."

The scene was quite familiar-looking outside my window as we passed the "pre-border." This time we did not have to stop. In an hour or so we would be back in Damascus and I would figure a way out then.

Suddenly, I was startled and brought back to reality by the sound of nonstop gunfire up ahead. "Ahmad," I asked, "what's going on? Do you see anything?"

"We are coming up on that same military checkpoint again and the sound is coming from around there," he said frantically.

"Please be careful, Ahmad," I said. "You need to slow down so we can figure out where the shelling is coming from." Once again I shoved you and your sister down to the taxi floor and asked you to play there for a while. *This is not good. What else can go wrong?* I thought.

We could now see the military vehicles lined up on either side of the highway. But rather than slowing down, all of a sudden Ahmed began to speed up towards them. I did not know what he was thinking, if he was thinking at all.

"Ahmad, slow down," I must have yelled. But he kept going faster as we approached the vehicles. He kept saying things in Arabic that I could not understand. Had he gone crazy? Was he going to just drive past them without stopping?

I yelled for him to slow down and told him that they would shoot at us if he didn't. "Please, Ahmad, slow down," I pleaded. I could see one soldier in the middle of the road waiting for us to slow down and it must have appeared to him that we were not going to do that. He fired a shot in the air that woke up Ahmad from his crazy stunt and he came to a screeching stop that made the car go sideways for a few feet.

The soldier pointed his gun at the windshield and slowly approached the car while a few more soldiers made themselves visible and followed suit. "Are you crazy?" the soldier yelled at Ahmad in Arabic. "Why are you driving so fast? Do you not see that this is a checkpoint? Get out of the car now," he ordered him.

I had not been that scared in a long time. I really thought we were going to be shot. Once again Ahmad got himself out of a jam and, after verifying our licenses and the contents of our trunk, we were let go.

Slowly this time, Ahmad drove past the parked vehicles. As I looked out the window, I saw three blood-covered bodies lined up in between two vehicles. And a few more feet past, yet another three bodies, lying motionless with bloody faces that reminded me of execution-style shootings. Thank God you and your sister were not exposed to that gory scene. You were still on the floor of the taxi. But it'll be a long time before I can forget those images.

My anger was overflowing and I didn't know who to direct it towards. I felt like punching Ahmad in the face right in front of his son for pulling such a dangerous stunt that might have killed us. I wanted to yell at someone. No, I wanted to kill someone, anyone, who was going to get in my way. *I am getting my girls out of this hell,* I vowed.

We finally made it back to Damascus and that is when I instructed Ahmad to take us back to my cousin Amir's office to figure out what our options were. There I learned of the events that had taken place with him while we were gone. Amir told me that a secret service unit contacted him regarding our whereabouts.

He told me that someone must have given them information that led them to him, but he did not know who it might have been. He said that he had no choice but to confess that, in fact, we had stopped by his office and that I had my girls with me. I didn't know how to react to what I was hearing except to listen and wait for what he might recommend afterwards. He said that he did not tell them where we might be headed but thought that they figured it out and probably called the border to alert them. He asked what I wanted to drink.

"Got any poison?" I jokingly responded.

I didn't want to tell him about the misspelling of your name mishap; he looked pretty distraught already. Besides, I take full responsibility for that, I should have stressed more about that since middle names are not commonly used in Syria.

"One option you have," he went on to tell me, "is to go into hiding for a few days in Damascus until we come up with another plan. However, the down side to that is that you are going to be pursued by police and the consequences might be more than you are willing to gamble with. My recommendation," he said, "is to simply take the girls back to their mother prior to the twenty-four-hour window that you still have and make up a story that you just wanted to spend the day with them. They really don't have a case on you as I see it," he added.

As I gathered from Amir, Jamal was still in Damascus taking care of some things. I gave him a call and he came back to meet with us and we made a decision to take you and your sister back to Alfouhila and there we would contact your mother to pick you up. The plan was simple enough, but the idea that there might be police waiting for us concerned me. Not because I was afraid of what might happen to me but what might happen to Jamal if they found him involved in the plan. I did not want anything to happen to him, and on the way back I assured him that I would take full responsibility for everything should they question him.

It was not long after we went through Damascus that I got a call from your mother. Surprisingly, she was not yelling or panicking. She asked me where I was, like nothing had happened, but I knew better. She asked if you and your sister were with me and when she could expect us to return. I told her that I wanted to spend the day with both of you and that I was just headed back to Alfouhila to have you spend some time with your friends there and to see your Aunt Mariam.

She began to tell me that she knew what I had done and that she knew I had tried to smuggle you across the Lebanese border. I quickly denied it and told her that she did not know what she was talking about. I was not in the mood to really talk with her or be interrogated by her, or anyone else for that matter. I was prepared for whatever came my way to keep you and your sister from going back to your dangerous residence in Homs.

Your mother said that she could have had the border patrol arrest me on the spot, but said that she understood the desperation of a father to protect his children and that if I brought you back, she would not file any charges against me.

Little did she know that I was ready for any battle with her or anyone else. I told her that I would call her when we got to our destination and she could pick you up then. I hung up the phone. I can almost see her smiling as though she had won a battle. She is shallow in that regard. *What battle has she won?* I thought. *The fact that she is gambling with her children's lives, or just the idea of getting under my skin? Either way, it does not matter. She will not succeed.*

I was curious about my cousin Zaid and called him to meet me at my sister's house upon my arrival. There he informed me of the chaos that ensued after I left him with your grandparents. He said that they accused him of being a part of the plan and threatened him with the police if he did not confess where we were. Furthermore, they had called the Congresswoman who is your mother's aunt and she was able to call on the authorities to locate our whereabouts.

Zaid said that there were roadblocks and checkpoints all the way to my residence in Alfouhila, checking every vehicle for us. Then they came to my sister's house and did a search there and threatened her in the same fashion to tell them where we might be hiding. I felt really bad for what everyone had gone through because of my actions, but sadly, I did not feel guilty at all.

I had to do whatever I had to do, I thought. There were no police present. I had you say goodbye to your cousins and that was when I told my cousin to take you back to his house where your mother was going to pick you both up.

"Daddy has to go back to America in a couple of days and I will not be able to see you for a while after today," I explained to you and your sister.

I promised you that I would be back soon for your birthdays that summer and assured you that I loved you both very much and that I would continue to call you and check up on you every week. Seeing you go into my cousin's taxi broke my heart and the feeling in my stomach felt like a furnace ready to explode. But in my mind I was already thinking of my next attempt to get you out, *Next time,* I thought, *nothing is going to stop me.*

Job

There once was a man in the land of Uz
Blameless and upright and the one he would choose
Seven sons and three daughters were born to him
They feasted daily but their future was dim
On a day with the lord, Satan came along
"I was roaming the earth where you say I belong"
Have you considered my servant job?
There is no one like him on the entire globe
Blameless and upright and fears the lord.
"Yes, but clearly because to him you afford"
You've given him in abundance and lives by your grace.
But put forth thy hand and he'll curse thee to thy face
God gave Satan the power over all things that job would own
"Do unto him as you please, only leave him alone."
One day a messenger came to Job and said;
"All your oxen, sheep, donkeys and servants are dead."
Just about that time, yet another messenger came to call.
"Great winds came upon your children and consumed them all."
Then Job tore off his robe and shaved his head.
He fell to the ground and boldly said
Naked I came from my mother's womb
The lord gave me and caused me to bloom
Naked I shall return, "Blessed be thy name"
And through it all, God; he did not blame.

Chapter 17

Fourth trip to Syria

Coming back to America this time was the worst thus far. I boarded the flight to Turkey with concern and caution. The thought of someone shooting it down was not far from my mind, as the airport was now the target for the opposing militant groups in Syria. I couldn't help but look at all of the passengers on board and wonder if any one of them was in a similar situation to mine. I'm sure, just from the looks on their faces, that they were just as concerned or worried about the situation in Syria and their loved ones.

I met the man who sat next to me and got a chance to pick his brain. This is something I often do when I encounter an elder of any race. I love to hear stories of wisdom. He asked me about my trip to Syria and what I was doing there. I tried to be vague and told him I was just visiting some relatives. I began to ask him about his trip and before long he told me his life's history. I did not mind it, but honestly, I would fade for moments at a time, thinking of you and your sister, as he kept sharing stories of his many businesses and how much money he had accumulated over the years. He had married four wives and had sixteen children. Jokingly, I asked if he knew all of their names. Surprisingly, he did and named them all for me.

He asked if I had any children and I began to tell him about you and your sister. Something about him made me comfortable about asking for his opinion on my situation. I began to tell him my story about how your mother had deceived me and ended up in Syria. I'm not sure why I felt the need to unload such personal information, but for some reason, as I began to talk, a certain calm came over me. After hearing my frustration, he asked if he could share a story with me.

It was a story of a most famous king. This king had everything a man could wish for under the sun. He had everything except the one thing he desired most. And that was to have a son. This king lived many years and while he could have married another woman who might have borne him a son, he chose not to and stayed with the same woman. One day while his wife was strolling around the castle, she went into the barn and from exhaustion, she just fell asleep.

Just about that same time, a thief entered the barn with the intention of stealing and found the queen sleeping. He hid from sight, and as he did, the Queen was visited by two angels who hovered around her. One of the angels whispered to her saying, "You will soon be blessed with a son that your husband has so patiently waited for, and he will be born to you on this day and that hour. And that same day a serpent will come crawling in and it will kill your son, for this is what is written."

After the angels vanished from sight, the thief, having overheard this, decided to steal no more. He would now wait until that fateful day and be the hero and protect that child from the deadly serpent.

So the day came and the Queen gave birth to a beautiful baby boy. The thief had been prepared with a sharp sword and made his way into the palace, waiting for that serpent. As the Queen was with her child, a large serpent was crawling and making its way to her room.

The thief notices it, and with his sword drawn, he rushes toward it, raises his sword and slices it right in half. However the powerful serpent's other half continues to rush towards the boy and kills him instantly, just like the angels said it would do.

"If you are meant to be with your daughters," the man told me, "and it is written, then so it will be."

I arrived in Turkey and made my way to a Starbucks coffee spot that I was now very familiar with. I had a waiting period of five hours before I would head back to America. So many things were going on in my head but mostly my body was numb. I ordered a large latte and sat down to rest a while. A young lady of color sat across from me and engaged me in conversation. She had an unusual accent and I could not figure out where she might be from.

She asked if I was going to America. I said I was. She said that she had family there, in Nevada, and she was also going there. We talked about many things, mostly about our different cultures and the politics that played a role in her home country of Ethiopia. We swapped stories of what was going on in Syria and the many deaths taking place and the thousands who continued to die yearly in her country. She said that she was thankful to an American missionary group that came to her country and talked with her about Jesus Christ and how it changed her life.

I typically like the discussion of religion and politics, but I was not in the mood then. I just listened to her and could not help but wonder about my own faith and whether I still believed in Christ as I had before. If God was testing me, I thought, He would probably be very disappointed with my current evil thoughts. My flight was now nearing and to be polite, I asked the young lady for her name.

"My name is Tigist," she said.

"That is a beautiful name, what does it mean?" I asked her.

"It means 'patience,'" she replied.

In America, I was now a different man. If I had lost interest in things previously, it was now tenfold. Every hour of everyday I was thinking about you and your sister. Things on the news were of no comfort, as every morning I would awake to the tally of deaths in Syria and how things were getting worse. At that point over sixty thousand lives had been lost and that number may be a low estimate. Letters I had sent to Senators Boxer and Feinstein and prominent figures were in vain. The responses I got were more than likely written by some intern who could care less about an issue that was too sensitive for any politician to touch.

There was no one I could count on to help me with getting you and your sister back. I had to just sit back and wait for another opportunity to go back to Syria in the summer and see what happened.

Life can be funny at times. All my life I have tried to do what's right. At sixteen I remember that I was going through a personality change. I was working at my father's store part time while I went to school. I was not very popular with girls due to my lack of confidence. I was just the nice guy they all liked as a friend. I tried to blend in by rebelling like the rest of the popular boys and I started smoking. That gave me a little boost in confidence and made me feel more of an adult. I really did not have a role model to speak of. Everyone in my family had their own life to worry about and having man-to-man talks with my dad was close to impossible.

My father was an old-fashioned man who was the only son of his parents. He was a great man and did everything for his family in terms of being a provider, but in the way of preparing me for what life was like in America, that was another issue and one he was not well informed about.

I wanted more than anything to be different than the rest of the family. One day I was given a special cigarette that one of our customers at the store wanted me to try. He told me that it was going to make me feel good. Just like the pills someone once gave me to try out when I was much younger. I was young and very gullible. After going home one night, I decided to try it. Turns out it was a marijuana joint laced with a chemical and it made me very sick. The whole family was worried that I may not recover from the crazy things this cigarette caused me to do.

After going to the hospital and being brought back to the house, I began to think about my life and what it all meant. Something emotional came out of that incident and caused me to fear death where, prior to that, it never even crossed my mind.

I began to think irrationally about the value of my life and whether it actually mattered to anyone if I lived or died. I was not thinking of or contemplating ending my life; to the contrary, I just wanted my life to mean something to someone.

I thought of my brothers and sisters and wondered how long it would be before they all got married and started focusing on their own lives and children. I thought that if God ever wanted to punish me one day, it would not be financially or physically. He would simply keep me from having a child of my own. Now that was a punishment I could not bear.

I'm not sure why I was afraid of that or where the idea originated from, but it occupied my mind for many years to come. And the picture became more real as I officially, and by my own consent, confirmed my Christianity with the help of a dear friend. I began to fear God as I became aware of the wrong choices I would make as an adult. Reading the Bible became almost a daily routine.

I felt empowered by its vast knowledge of wisdom, stories of average men who became kings, and powerful kings who ended up losing everything, including their souls, by deviating from the word of God.

So, now, here I was, contemplating things in my head that were not only ungodly but were criminal. This was not me. These things that were going through my mind were simply thoughts of desperation and I must control them. I knew that getting you out of the country legally was no longer an option, at least right then. What would you and your sister think of me if I were to go through with the plan I had in my mind? After all, what was life really worth, living in fear? I thought.

For the next few months, I would cash my checks and take a portion of them in cash to prepare for my next trip to Syria. This time I would need more money for more bribes and possibly weapons that were very expensive and almost impossible to get. I would have to hire a group of guys for protection and guides to help me cross the border into Turkey or Lebanon. *This time around, I will not come back without you, God willing,* I told myself.

My plan was not concrete, and it would need refining and tuning once I got there. I would not involve anyone who had helped me in the past. I would simply find a group of guys I could trust who could use some money and somehow take you and your sister by force. I would then go into hiding for a few days until the right time came and then we would make our escape.

Many names and faces came to mind who might get hurt in the process, but in the back of my mind, I was hoping that it would not come to that. I would make sure that at least your mother and her parents did not get hurt; I did not want that on my conscience.

Before going to sleep each night, I would pray that something miraculous would take place and your mother would simply call and say that she was bringing you back. That would not happen, of course. The anger grew inside of me and more and more I was making the commitment to go through with the plan. My mind kept telling me that I would be blameless for doing this, but my heart was aching with shame at what I was turning into.

Where did I go wrong? What did I do to cause this? How can I be so foolish as to let your mother do this to us? I kept looking for answers wherever I could find them. I researched a similar case of a father who took his kids from America to Syria and how the mother did everything to get them back. After many years apart, the father finally made a mistake and came back to America to resolve some personal business issues and was captured by police as he entered the country. After much negotiation, the kids were finally reunited with their mother. That was not going to be the case for me; your mother would not attempt that.

The time was now approaching for me to travel to Syria and see you again. I gave notice at my work and found that I had no vacation time left.

I was informed that it was possible for me to borrow up to two weeks of vacation time from the upcoming year. That was all I needed, I thought.

A week before I would have to travel to Syria, I decided to do something I had been contemplating for a long time. I decided that I was going to get a tattoo. I told the artist the story of the brave frog that decided to jump out of the boiling water before it died and asked him to come up with a drawing that would depict the story. A day later I visited him and was impressed with what he had come up with. Ten hours later, I was very pleased and could not wait to go to Syria and show it to you.

I packed my bags and was to fly out of LAX around the end of June, 2012, and hopefully get there before your birthdays on the 1st of July. I've never been more thankful that both of your birthdays fall on the same day than I was then. I called my cousin Zaid in Syria to pick me up at the airport in Damascus once I got there, but that was it. I promised to not use him or endanger him after that on the trip.

Fallen Soldier

Have you heard the news today?
A star has fallen from the horizon.
If there ever was a day to wish upon a fallen star,
This is the star and today is the day.
Have you ever noticed a sky so dark?
Or the moon, hanging low and dim?
Even the birds have a more somber tone,
And there is a hole in our hearts where he left his mark.
The wind died down,
The trees and waters, they lay still;
And a deafening silence echoes in our minds.
For a brave soldier has fallen,
Whose name, will forever be around.
You can see it in his eyes,
And drawn upon his face
He was on a mission, and the mission was accomplished.
He is now with our lord, in a warm embrace.

Dedicated to my cousin, Elias

Chapter 18

I was anxious to get to Syria as I boarded the flight to Dubai and then to Damascus. Flights from Turkey into Syria were no longer available since both countries were now on bad terms. I didn't care about that too much. As a matter of fact, it was to my advantage that way. It would mean that crossing the border into Turkey might be easier when there was chaos than crossing at a formal border crossing. I had prepared myself mentally to deal with the typical travel incidents along the way and the trip was uneventful for the most part.

I arrived at Damascus International Airport and was rushed by obnoxious baggage handlers who usually work together to get the most money out of travelers. I was not moved or shook up by them this time. This time I was more in control and I enjoyed the fact that they were fighting to help with my baggage. I even encouraged some of them to join in. I generously tipped each one of them and was not at all upset. I was greeted by my cousin Zaid. I did notice that the airport was more tightly guarded this time around.

Driving through the streets of Damascus was emotional this time around. It seemed that the militant groups had made their way into the capital and caused extensive damage in the past few months. The buildings that I had passed along the way many times before now showed signs of mortar fire and bombs.

It was an uneasy feeling to see a once beautiful and historic capital in a state of war and destruction. Mosques that were once iconic and had stood the test of time for over a thousand years were now all but rubble.

I just wanted to close my eyes and just get to our destination a couple of hours away. There were many more roadblocks and a greater military presence on this trip, which caused long lines while everyone waited patiently for vehicles to be searched. It had become a normal way of life for most drivers. I wondered if things would ever go back to normal in this country.

My cousin Zaid was brave for driving all the way to Damascus to pick me up and I was grateful for that. I could have possibly taken a taxi but you never know who you are getting a ride from. "Things are different now," Zaid said. He informed me that one of my cousin's husbands had recently disappeared and that I should be very careful on this trip. He went on to tell me that there were many cases like that all across the country. "The militant groups are kidnapping random people and asking for a ransom to fund their cause," he told me. "They don't care who it is as long as they think his family has money."

"How long has my cousin's husband been missing?" I asked.

"Almost a month," he said. "Some people just go shopping and never return."

We had a chance to talk about my previous trip. Zaid told me that after I left for America, people were talking about the incident for weeks. He said that everyone in our village had much respect for me for what I tried to do for my children. He warned me, however, to be extra cautious if I were to try something like that again. "The Syrian police and army are not very tolerant these days towards anyone who breaks the law," he said. "They shoot first and ask questions later."

I nodded my head, acknowledging what he was saying, but the first thought that came to mind was the plan I had and the guns I would seek to purchase. *I guess it will not be as easy as I had hoped for,* I thought. I didn't want to hear any more from my cousin. Even though what he had told me was very valuable, I just didn't want the reality to set in that my plan was not going to be easily executed.

We arrived in my hometown of Alfouhila around 9pm and I asked Zaid to drop me off at my sister's vacant home where I would take up residence for the short time I was in Syria. There was much to do and much to think about.

I called another sister, Mariam, to let her know I had arrived and I told her that I would stop by the next morning for coffee. Her husband was now with her from America and was hoping that the U.S. Embassy would grant them paperwork to take the whole family to America.

I was glad that your Uncle Diab was there; he always gave me comfort whenever I was down on myself. I met them for coffee the next morning and was very happy to see my sister was still in good spirits, in spite of the problems I caused her on my last trip. This time would be different. I would not get her or anyone else involved. This time it would be strictly about getting the job done.

We began to talk about you and your sister and she asked me when I would be seeing you. I said that I would be talking to your mother in a couple of hours and make arrangements. She told me that there were some rumors flying around that your grandparents were seeking paperwork to leave Syria soon and possibly going to see their son in Guatemala. That did not bother me but I acted like I was listening. She said that there was something else. I looked at her as her tone of voice changed.

"They are not going alone," she said. "They are thinking of taking your daughters with them."

I could not believe what I was hearing. "Who the hell are they to decide what to do with my children and where to take them? And is their mother going there, too?"

"I'm not sure," she said.

My mind started to wonder and all I could think at that point was that I needed to act fast if my plan was going to work.

I called your mother and made arrangements to see you. We had a chance to discuss many things regarding the current situation in Syria and the violence that was now widespread across the country. Once there were areas unaffected by violence; now no one was safe. Your mother was still working and living in Damascus while you and your sister were still in that dreaded town of Alhafar with your grandparents. I was told that your grandparents' home in Homs, where you had lived, had been ransacked and was now occupied by a militant group.

Your grandparents used to show off and brag about that house and how much it was worth; I guess nothing lasts forever. I noticed that your mother's tone was different these days.

The desperation, regret and violence she was experiencing were now taking a toll on her thinking and also on her parents. One thing for sure,

I did not trust anything your mother had to say, unfortunately. She was good at getting sympathy from those around her, but I always had to read between the lines with her.

She informed me that it was getting very dangerous for her to be in Damascus and that she had been subjected to many bombings in the building where she worked. She said that things were scary and she was now more concerned about the safety of her family, as well as the future of the country. It seems that the government-opposing groups were getting stronger and had no mercy or agenda. They were simply doing anything destructive they could to shake and destabilize the current regime.

Over the last few months, the current President had made many concessions and even rewritten the constitution in order to appease the overwhelming demands of his citizens. He abolished the current House of Representatives and appointed a new and improved group of men and women from various religious sects to help in balancing the power and possibly give him more support. He fired many of the prominent men in power and replaced them with either Sunni Muslim leaders or Christians.

But all of that was in vain. While this war started with citizens concerned about corruption and lack of freedom, it surely was not about that now. This war was now only serving to destroy, weaken and destabilize the country. The only ones who stood to gain from this were many countries that wanted to control Syria's vast resources.

The more we talked about things in the country, the more optimistic I became that she might be thinking of leaving it. But I needed to know where she was thinking of going. I did not want to share with her the rumors I had gathered from my sister and I wanted her to mention it first. She said that she had talked her parents into leaving Syria and going to America to stay with their son in California. And that life for them in Syria was getting difficult, given their health problems, the danger of traveling on open roads, and lack of medical care.

I was listening to see when she was going to talk about you and your sister and your role in all of this. She finally got to it and asked me what I thought of her parents taking you both with them. With your mother, things are not cut and dried. There is always an ulterior motive. So I had to be careful about how to respond to that.

Calmly I asked, "Why would they go with their grandparents if their father is here and can take them back to their own home in America?" I couldn't wait for her answer.

"Because I'm not ready to let them go yet; my parents won't be ready to leave for a couple months," she said.

I was trying to be calm, but I could feel my blood boiling. "Why would you want to keep them here even for a minute longer? Things are really bad here and kidnappings are a normal thing now. Why would we subject our children to that possibility when I can take them with me? Think about what you're saying. I am their father and it is my responsibility to care for them if you decide to stay here."

The conversation was not going anywhere. All I wanted to do at that point was to arrange for a time to see you. She said that what I needed to do was to meet you and your sister at a pastor's home in the same town. I would have to again give him my passport to hold and only see you both for a couple hours.

Your birthday was in five days and I did not want to ruin my chance of seeing you freely. So I agreed, and the next day I met you both at the pastor's home. He and his wife were very gracious and hospitable. I brought over some toys that you had asked me for and we spent a couple hours together. However, all I could think about was how quickly I could get a group of guys together and get this over with.

I went back to Alfouhila and wanted to stop by and say hello to my cousin's Uncle Jamal and see how he was doing. He asked me if I was going to make another attempt. I did not want to share any information with him, not because of a trust issue, but I just felt bad for what he went through for my sake the last time around. I just told him that I was hoping your mother would come to her senses and allow me to take you back with me. He said, "*Inshalla*." (God willing). "Just be careful," he added. "In case you decide to do anything, I'm here for you."

Finding a group of guys was going to be difficult because I would have to leave my comfort zone of working with people I knew and trusted. But it had to be done. There was a neighboring village close by that I would get fresh meat from. Rayan was a small Sunni Muslim village and, over the years, they had always gotten along with our predominantly Christian town. It was a mutual business agreement. They come to our town for certain shopping needs and we did the same.

The butcher seemed like a nice guy every time we met. We became acquainted as he would put aside the best part of the cow or calf for me. I met with him and began to talk about things as he was cutting the fresh meat into little chunks in preparation for the birthday party I was planning for you and your sister.

He would have to get our portion out of two or three cows when it was all said and done. Even though I was still not sure that your mother would allow me to be with you and bring you with me to Alfouhila to celebrate there. I guess I was being optimistic.

In a subtle way I began to share with him my story about you and your sister and my dilemma. "I'm running out of options," I said. "Do you have any suggestions that can possibly help me?" I was hoping he would tell me what I wanted to hear. That he might have a few guys he could recommend.

He was quiet as he cut into that meat. "What do you have in mind?" he asked.

I was almost shaking as I wanted to blurt out what was on my mind, but I had to be careful. In this country, there are a lot of secret police and informants who can be normal people like doctors and teachers and yes, even butchers. "I guess I'm just looking for a couple guys to hang out with me for protection and possibly guide me through the streets, as I may be doing some traveling," I said.

"Is that all?" he asked. "That seems simple enough; I have the perfect men for that. These guys are my cousins and they are currently on leave from duty. They are normally working as traffic police, but with the current situation in Homs, they are afraid of going to work. So they would love to be of assistance."

This is too good to be true, I thought. *Now I don't have to worry about purchasing guns and subjecting myself to illegal and dangerous activity.* I told him that in a few days, I would possibly have my girls come visit me in Alfouhila, as it was their birthday, and that I would need to meet with his cousins as soon as possible to discuss my travel needs and give them their assignments. I did not want to share any more information with him because I thought that if these men were unemployed, they would be easily enticed by money and I could then really tell them what I needed of them.

I went back home and was to prepare a barbecue with my sister and her husband. As we sat there talking, my brother in-law insisted on getting information from me about any plans to take you and your sister back to America. To be vague and still pacify his curiosity, I simply told him that it would be almost impossible to do so. That if I had a chance in a million, I would need their passports stamped with an Exit Visa, we would have to remove their names from the list at the border, and, of course, we would need them to be with me away from their mother.

"So, with all of those obstacles, you can see how it would be impossible", I said.

He just shook his head in disbelief and I felt that I got him off of my back for the time being. Then all of the sudden he said, "What if I tell you that I know someone who can help you with all of that."

I was all ears, but I said, "Believe me, I've tried everything and it's much harder than you think."

He gave me the name and phone number of his friend and I just put it in my pocket, not really having much faith in it. I was determined to go through with my plan. I had had enough of the nonsense over the last two years with either broken promises from your mother or failed attempts. I would now take the initiative and do it my way.

On the 28th of June, I met with two of my butcher's cousins alone at the house. I was a little scared, I must admit. I had no idea who these people really were and had no idea of how they might be able to take advantage of me and my situation. They looked like regular guys. They did not come in with uniforms, but I was not sure if they were armed. I offered them some coffee and some American smokes that they seemed to enjoy very much. I began to probe their background to see if I could trust them with sensitive information. So I asked them a hypothetical question. "If someone wanted to leave this country and take his children with him, and, let's say, he had some restrictions placed on him and his children, is there a way for him to cross the border without getting caught?"

They looked at each other and one said, "Depends on who this person is and who his daughters are."

I lied and said that I had a friend in America and his wife abducted his kids and brought them here to Syria and he was trying to get them back. "He wants to come here but before he does, he wants to know if there is someone who can help him," I told them.

They both laughed and one said, "My friend, with the right amount of money you can move a mountain across the border."

"Whatever you or your friend need, we are ready and, yes, we have the connections to get the job done," the other one said. "Tell us more about your friend and his situation."

"I will tell you all you need to know as soon as I talk with him, but for now I need you to do something for me," I told them. "I want to employ you both to be my guards for the duration of my vacation and I will let you know when I will be doing some traveling. You will make yourselves like ghosts. You cannot be seen with me, but whenever I need to take a taxi anywhere, you will follow and keep watch. I can pay you each one thousand dollars for two weeks of your services. I will give you each five hundred dollars up front and the rest in two weeks."

I felt safer now that I had someone to rely on should there be an unexpected opportunity to be with you and your sister. The plan was taking shape. Now I could focus and see what needed to be done next.

I called your mother and asked if I could see you the next day. She said that before I saw you again, she insisted on me making an appearance at her uncle's house and apologizing to him and to her parents for putting them through hell with my attempt to smuggle you and your sister across the Lebanese border on my last trip. She said that I almost gave her mother a heart attack and that her uncle was disappointed in me after he trusted me and made his home available for me to see you and your sister there.

I couldn't believe what I was hearing. *Is this woman sick or what,* I thought. "Are you fucking kidding me? You want me to apologize for trying to protect my girls from the bombings that were taking place? That is not going to happen," I said. "And furthermore, I will do it again and again if you and your family continue to put them in danger." I felt stronger now for some reason. I used to kiss her ass and take so much verbal abuse, just for the sake of being able to see you and your sister for a few hours, but now I was sure I would see you no matter what.

"Listen," I said. "I have been trying for the last two years to be on good terms with you for the sake of our girls. I have subjected myself to humiliation, embarrassment, disrespect, and financial ruin, not to mention almost being killed on several occasions. But this is it. I need to see my girls and they need to see their father."

I didn't want things to get ugly with your mother, but I had taken all I could take at that point. I guess my attitude was working. Her voice was now softer and she was listening for once. I told her that if anyone was going to travel with our daughters, it was going to be me.

"The time is now," I said. "Let's resolve whatever we need to and figure out what's in the best interest of the girls and get it over with because I have to be honest with you, if I don't take my girls with me to America on this trip, then it may take me years to come back here again and they will be your responsibility to deal with. My work will not allow me to leave anymore. My vacation time is over and, quite frankly, I am not in a financial position to travel every six months to come see them, either. So you need to make a decision, and I want you to know that I am okay either way."

I was hoping that with what I said, it would change the way your mother was dealing with me. Maybe this way she would think I was not as desperate to be with you and your sister as I really was and reverse the psychology a little in my favor. And wouldn't you know it, it worked. She began to speak and suggested that she had had enough of all the court hearings and lawyers and said that maybe we could resolve this on our own.

Although my time here was limited to two weeks, I had made a decision not to leave without you and your sister. I had already planned for that prior to leaving America. I had left a few signed checks back at home and some instructions for my friend in the event something happened to me. I knew that it was possible I could get hurt or even killed on this trip. I had set aside certain monies for you and your sister for college and other expenses when you made your way to America. I felt good about that. I did not want you to struggle in the future, should I not make it. I left you both some instructions and some life lessons I had learned along the way.

I needed to know if your living arrangement in Alhafar had changed since I was there last. And while the idea of apologizing to your grandparents was something I initially turned down, I had to swallow my pride and do just that in order to get information on you and your sister. I told your mother that I had no problem in meeting with her parents and uncle to apologize for what I had put them through.

Meanwhile, I decided to call my brother-in-law's contact and see what he had to say. Nessim had a very dry and rough voice. I introduced myself and told him that he was referred to me by my brother-in-law who thought that he could be of service to me. He immediately recognized my brother-in-law's name and was willing to speak to me. He asked what he could do for me.

I explained my situation to him and asked him specifically whether he could help with getting you and your sister legally out of the country with the set of obstacles that had hindered our attempts the last few times around. He was curious about the men who had helped me previously. I told him that I could not release that information and that it was irrelevant at that time.

He went on to tell me a little about the way he worked and his background. He said that he had successfully helped hundreds of people obtain Exit Visas and legal documents to travel all around the world and what I was asking for was going to be very difficult. He said that he had many connections in Syria, but because my case involved underage children, he would have to do some research and get back to me.

I was not disappointed with his answer since I really did not have faith in him to begin with. I was just using him for information, and if by chance he was able to help me, then by all means I was going to give him a chance. After all, it would not hurt to have a plan A, B, or even C.

At my sister Mariam's house, I made arrangements to have your birthday party held there. My sister asked if I was really going to pull it off and talk your mother into letting you be with me. I told her that I was optimistic and that it was better to be prepared, just in case. I knew what I had to do. And that was to pacify your mother by completing her request to make my appearance at her parent's house.

I bought some gifts and drove over to Alhafar and met with your mother and her wicked family. I was greeted and asked to come in. You and your sister were nowhere around. I figured that they wanted some privacy to speak their mind. I was prepared for anything, but I made a decision to be civil, no matter what they threw at me.

This family was notorious for exaggerations. They sat there, silent as one, waiting for an apology. I began by thanking them for taking care of you both and told them how appreciative I was for having them deal with a difficult situation. I was having a hard time finding the right words to express my disappointment in the way I had been treated, but eventually I got to the apology. I told them that I was sorry for putting them in a bad position on my last trip. I apologized to her uncle and told him how I would never forget his hospitality towards me and my girls.

"However, I will tell you this," I told them. "I am not ashamed or afraid to do whatever necessary to protect my girls, as I'm sure you also would do for your own children."

Your grandmother interrupted me and began to tell me how she had treated you and your sister like her own children. She reminded me of the crazy stunt I pulled on my last trip to kidnap you from their arms and shared with me what she did that week after you and your sister came back home. She said that once she felt that your lives were in danger going to that Christian school, she pulled you both out and a day later the school was bombed. "So, this should show you that I care about your children," she said.

I was listening to this crazy woman confess to me that you both came close to death and yet was claiming that she had saved your lives. I had no answer to that or a comment. I was simply sick to my stomach just listening.

I interrupted and changed the subject. "I'm asking that I take my daughters with me to Alfouhila to celebrate their birthday with their cousins tomorrow, as I am only here for another week," I told them.

The meeting was somewhat fruitful in that I was able to pick you and your sister up the next day and enjoy the celebration of your birthday. Part of me was still angry towards your mother for the humiliation, but I would live with it as long as it meant spending more time with you.

The next day I drove to Alhafar and picked you both up. With you both in my arms, and some close friends and family, we enjoyed the party. Of course, my mind was racing a million miles an hour. I wanted this day to be the day where I put you in a taxi and went into hiding, but my plan was not yet complete. I still needed to be cautious.

I was smoking a cigarette with the men when I received a call from Nessim. I excused myself and went into a bedroom to talk. He sounded very enthusiastic. He asked if I was still interested in proceeding with the plan. "Let me hear what you have to say," I said.

He began by telling me the worst case and best case scenarios. "It can be done," he said. "Here is what I need from you."

I was overly excited and as he kept talking and asking for certain things, I was even more excited, simply because most of what he was asking for was available and ready. However, time was of the essence if we were going to pull this off, he said.

"I need you to meet someone in Damascus tomorrow morning with all of the documents I asked for," he told me. "I will send you a taxi driver who will meet with you and drive you to a certain destination where you will meet with my contact and there you will give him all of the documents and also his fee. We will discuss the total fees thereafter. Do you understand everything I am telling you and do you understand that there is a risk involved?" he asked.

"Yes," I said. "I understand and I will meet with the driver tomorrow after I drop my girls off." We agreed to meet at 10am the next day.

A taxi pulled up next to my house the next day as agreed and I was ready with all of the documents. The first thing the man asked was if I had everything Nessim had asked for.

"Yes," I said.

He asked to see the money I was to give their contact and quickly put it under his seat. I had no idea who this guy was other than he was sent by Nessim. He didn't introduce himself and I was not about to ask. Maybe sometime on the drive there he would open up.

I didn't tell him just yet that we would be followed by my hired guards. But to make sure I was not being put together by these guys, I asked him to stop at the local store to pick up some cigarettes and at the same time find out if I could recognize the type of car my guards were following us with. A black car that seemed to be following us stopped across the street from the store, and as I exited the store, I noticed that it was them and was relieved that it was not a scam.

The driver was quiet for the most part as he decided to take the back way to Damascus, which meant he would have to go through the town of Alhafar. As he got close, I immediately reclined my seat and made myself disappear just long enough to pass through without any nosy person recognizing me headed to Damascus. The driver looked at me kind of strangely, like I was some kind of lunatic, and I just smiled and told him the reason.

The news on television that morning had not been comforting, as rebels were causing havoc around Damascus. But so far, our drive had been pretty safe. As we approached downtown Damascus, the driver called Nessim and informed him that we had arrived. He received information on whom and where to meet the man who was going to help me.

We drove through a circular intersection like I had only seen in the movies. That was where we were to meet this man. I was very nervous about the whole thing, but I was committed and was not going to back off now. The only thing that scared me more than anything was the fact that I had to give this total stranger every document that I had worked so hard to obtain, including your passports. What would happen if something went wrong and the authorities had to confiscate them? I would be in deep shit and all my work so far would go to waste.

The driver pulled next to some shops at the intersection and talked to someone about our location. Fifteen minutes later a man approached our car and got into the back seat. I briefly glanced at him to see what he looked like. He began to explain to the driver what had happened and told him that we needed to move fast, as there was going to be a shift change soon and his contact on the inside was expecting him as soon as possible. So the driver handed him all of my documents and also the money. I was speechless for a moment and was about to question what was happening, but I bit my tongue and hoped that they knew what they were doing.

I heard the man say that he would be about an hour or so and that he would meet us back here. I asked the taxi driver to walk with me and get a bite to eat while we waited for some good news.

We walked down the street and found ourselves in a little café. This café reminded me of scenes in old Syrian sit-coms where regulars attended daily. The air was filled with rich coffee aroma and hookah smoke. Each table had some sort of board game like backgammon, checkers or chess. I got a few stares from big mustached men, as I was sporting a pair of dark sunglasses and an outfit that screamed "American." I knew I stood out, but I kind of liked it. After all, I had bodyguards just around the corner. At least I hoped they were. I ordered a glass of the famous Damascus tea and sat there thinking of what could possibly happen in the next hour.

A few minutes passed and I noticed two men enter the café. They were my guards. They saw me but walked by and sat at a table next to us. For a minute I couldn't help but feel like I was in a movie. I felt proud for doing this and was hopeful that it would work and soon we would be in America and I would share this story with you.

The cell phone rang and the taxi driver stood up while talking to someone. He gave me the sign to go and I followed him outside. As we walked down the street he was still on the phone and I was full of anticipation. As we got close to our taxi, we noticed two policemen looking in through the windshield. My heart stopped for a minute, and I must say, I was pretty scared. I knew that there was a chance this could happen. No matter how much you anticipate trouble, it seems you are never fully prepared when it gets there.

I stopped walking briefly and waited for my driver to go over and talk with the policemen. I was about thirty feet away and pretended to look at some watches outside of a jewelry store.

My guards were slowly walking towards our car as the driver was engaged in a conversation with the two policemen. It turned out that he was illegally parked and they asked him to move the car immediately. And while this was a big relief, I was still pretty shook up.

After the driver got in the car, I followed suit and we decided to circle the intersection while waiting for our contact. I finally asked the driver about the phone call and what had just taken place. He said that the man was coming back with our documents and that he had been unable to get them stamped. I was extremely disappointed but now more concerned about my documents. I knew how valuable American passports were to someone in this country, especially with the current situation. I had heard of stories where they were selling stolen passports for thousands of dollars, and at this point, I just wanted my stuff back.

We circled the intersection three times before finally spotting the contact. He entered the car and tried to explain how difficult our situation was. It seems that people were being extra-cautious these days doing favors that could lead to an investigation.

Our contact said that he had an idea. He suggested that he keep the passports until the following day and that he knew someone else who could possibly get the job done. My driver called Nessim right away with the news. But my gut feeling told me to just take my documents and deal with this on my own.

Nessim asked to speak to me and asked if I was comfortable with this man's suggestion. I told him that I was not. I got my documents while my driver asked the man for our money back. Nessim took a hundred dollars out of it and gave it to him for his trouble and we decided to head back home.

Once again the thought of failure was knocking. I couldn't help but feel frustrated and I could not understand why I was facing so many dead ends. I began to talk to God in my head and ask why he was not making this easy for me. *Is there something I'm missing here?* I asked myself. *Is there something beyond my understanding that is telling me to stop trying and just accept the fact that you and your sister are meant to stay here in this country?* I just could not buy into it, but I had to keep trying.

The drive back gave me much time to reflect on all of my options thus far. I began to think of all of the negotiations with your mother, her lawyer, the Archbishop and her family and tried to find something that I perhaps missed or had not tried. I knew that her parents were probably tired of being tied down with two children who were not their responsibility. I knew that they would rather be in America with their own sons rather than to be stuck in this war-torn country. So the only possible conclusion was that they needed money.

I was not going to give up on getting you out illegally, but I thought that maybe I could convince your mother to come up with some sort of settlement that we could both live with. After all she had mentioned the other day that she wanted to find a solution away from all of the legal courts. *Yes, I think I will try that approach.* I just took a deep breath and decided to relax for the rest of the drive.

With so many attempts at getting those passports stamped and attempts to get your names removed from restricted travel status, I gave up hope and focused solely on smuggling you by car across the border. At what border, I had no clue, but it was the only option left. But before I made that final decision and possibly put you and me in danger, I had to try a final peaceful solution with your mother. And if that did not work, I would once again be blameless for whatever action I decided to take to get us out.

Before I talk to your mother, I usually take a few minutes to pace around the house. I prepare tea and make sure I have a pack of cigarettes and I mentally prepare for her unreasonable demands and then make the phone call.

The next morning that is what I did again. I called her and we began with the usual small talk that I normally hate and slowly we got to the proposal I had in mind.

I wanted her to feel like she was in charge and I reminded her to please forget about our personal differences and our legal battles and just focus on a solution that had you and your sister's best interests at heart. She listened as I asked her to be fair and ask for anything that would make her comfortable with me taking you both with me to America.

It seemed that she was prepared for such a question when demand after demand began rolling off of her tongue with not a stutter. The first thing she said was that she wanted the equivalence of half the value of my house in America in cash. Then she began to take inventory of what furniture we had, cars, bank accounts, investments, art on the walls, all the way down to the table covers that she said all belonged to her and she then placed a value on all of that and came up with the sum that she would settle for. Next she wanted me to drop the legal suit I had filed against her in America regarding child abduction orders and to clear her of all wrongdoing. She wanted me to agree to a divorce and she wanted to have, in writing, an agreement for joint custody of you and your sister. And, finally, once she decided to move back to America, I would have to agree to have you and your sister live with her as your primary residence.

I listened to all her demands but my mind was elsewhere. As a matter of fact, the demands, while they were ridiculous and unreasonable, did not cause me to put up much resistance. I would interject every few seconds just to make her feel like I was listening. But part of me had no faith in her ever going through with any of it other than her wanting to squeeze as much money from me as possible. I knew that she had an agenda or an ulterior motive just from previous broken promises she had made. Nonetheless I entertained the idea.

"Our house is not worth much," I told her. "The real estate market in America at this point would value our house for just about what we owe on it, therefore it does not have any equity. Second, the cars we own either have an outstanding loan or are not worth much. And, finally, the furniture and other things you mentioned are hardly worth talking about. As a matter of fact, you can have them all, including your valuable table covers.

"Now with all that said," I asked, "what amount of money would you agree to?"

She paused and threw a number out that she knew full well I would struggle to get. The number was in the thousands, and she had never earned a dollar nor ever saved a dollar for the household as long as we had been married, but I still agreed to it without hesitation.

As for the other demands that were more important to me – like dropping the charges of child abduction and agreeing to a divorce and her possibly going back to America and having to deal with these issues again – they really bothered me.

Now that I had at least come to the conclusion of her demands, I could begin to have a renewed faith in possibly leaving with you and your sister legally and with her consent and the Syrian court's consent. And there would be no need for crossing borders or paying thousands of dollars to men to smuggle us out. I figured that, while her financial demands were much greater than it would cost me to smuggle you out, at least it would be like killing a dozen birds with one stone.

For starters, she would have to give her permission to the Syrian court to lift the travel restriction on both of you. Second, she would have to surrender all of your documents that are essential for us to all travel legally through the Syrian international airport. Third, I would finally be free from my marriage to her and not have to deal with her or her wicked family ever again. And finally, I would be done with the court hearings in America and be able to live in peace with you and your sister.

Things in the country were so bad at this point that I had no choice but to agree to all of these demands. She had me in a corner and she knew it. It was simply Blackmail 101. She had no care in the world about whether her demands would put a financial strain on our future. Nor that her delaying our departure would possibly put us in danger of ever leaving, due to the threats to bomb the airports. She was only concerned about how much she could get away with. It was not only heartless, it was sad. I could not fathom how a sane mother who was educated and knew the dangers that were imposed on us every second could be so selfish.

I was disgusted, to say the least. But I wanted to make sure I understood the demands perfectly and I repeated them back to her and asked if I had missed anything. She simply said no and I made her a promise that I would meet all of the demands, beginning with me contacting my lawyer the next morning and having him withdraw and drop the case entirely against her. I told her I would have my attorney mail the paperwork to her brother in California so that she was a hundred percent sure it was done.

Second, I told her that, regarding the money she was asking for; I would have a friend of mine meet with her brother in America and give him part of the money, since I did not have the means to give it all to her in Syria. As for the rest, I would give to her whatever cash I could before I left and whatever remained to be paid I would give to her in monthly payments. Of course she wanted all of it in writing and notarized. I agreed once again.

Third, I would have to agree to the custody arrangement. That would be a little tricky. I will get to that later.

Calling my lawyer was one of the hardest things I've had to do. It seemed that the only card I was holding on your mother in order to have some leverage was now about to disappear. I thought about it for a little while, only because I knew her very well. And my lawyer had advised against this idea once before. She could easily back off on her end of the bargain once she was released from the obligation to appear in court for child abduction in America.

She could also do the same once her brother received the money. I had a sick feeling in my stomach about the whole thing, but for some reason I could not stop myself from doing it. I had absolutely no other choice if I wanted to leave this country safely and before it was too late.

Many thoughts crossed my mind about what I would do if she were to renege on our agreement. Of course every thought was worse than the previous one and I did not have time to waste thinking of the worst. I decided to give her the benefit of the doubt this time and proceeded to contact my lawyer that same evening, which would make it around ten in the morning in America.

I got lucky and reached him before he had to be in court. I shared the latest news with him and asked him to go to court to withdraw and dismiss all charges against your mother and to also add some stipulations regarding her visitation with you and your sister should she ever go back to America. He was not happy with this request and tried to talk me out of it.

I explained that your mother was leaving me no choice but to do it. "If this does not work, I have only myself to blame," I said.

He assured me that he would do as I asked and that he would email me with the court order and also send a copy to your mother's brother.

Meanwhile I called my friend in America and asked him to meet with her brother and arrange to give him the agreed amount in cash and to sign a letter stating that he was receiving the money on behalf of his sister. I further asked him to state in the letter that should I and my girls fail to arrive in America by a certain date, the money would be returned immediately.

Once I made those two phone calls, I felt a sense of relief. I'm not sure why, but I did. I guess in a way I was clearing my conscience, knowing full well that I had utilized the peaceful route first before the alternative. *This way people will know my good intentions, God forbid something were to happen to me,* I thought. I looked to the heavens and spoke to God, saying, "Now, Lord, it's in your hands."

Sleeping was completely out of the question that night. I was pacing all over the place awaiting an email from my lawyer and an answer from my friend. I waited until midnight before I got an email stating that the request had been filed with the courts and that by the next afternoon it would be emailed to me and her brother for review.

The next morning I spoke with my friend and was told that he was meeting with the brother to give him the money. At that point I was now ready to talk to your mother and share the news.

I had not finished my thought that morning when I received a phone call that would not only change things, but would turn everything upside down. It was a call from Nessim. He sounded a bit out of breath as he talked to me. Now, I had not yet met Nessim in person, but I could tell from his breathing that he might be a big guy. He began to tell me the latest developments and was now confident that our plan would work one hundred percent.

My biggest and most troubling obstacle thus far had been the travel restriction placed on you and your sister on all borders of Syria. With that in place, we were unable to move across the border without being stopped or arrested. Nessim seemed to have found a solution for that. He said that he had found the right source to remove the restriction for twenty-four hours – possibly up to forty-eight hours, depending on how fast we could move. That meant that if we decided to proceed and removed the restriction on a Thursday, it would give us the whole day to cross the border without a problem. And since all government offices close on Fridays, it would extend our window of opportunity by another twenty-four hours.

The thing to keep in mind, he said, was that once I gave him the green light, I would not be able to back off unless I forfeited the money it was going to cost. While the amount was less than I had thought it would be, it was still a lot of money.

I did not tell Nessim about the deal I had made with your mother yet. I was keeping my options open, just in case one of the two plans fell apart. So, there I was, faced with the possibility of two plans to get us out when just a few days ago I had been on the verge of giving up. *This*, I thought, *is too good to be true.*

A lot of things were happening too fast and my mind was on overload. Where should I put all of my focus? I was thinking of my lawyer in America, the meeting with her brother and my friend, the deal your mother and I had made and now this news from Nessim. Not to mention my own plan to smuggle you out illegally on my own. With all of that going on at the same time, you would think I would be stressed out. But to the contrary, I felt very much at ease and in control.

I took a deep breath and told Nessim that I would give him my final answer in a couple of days and to keep everyone in check until then.

Meanwhile I had to talk to your mother about the news from my lawyer in America. I called her and gave her the news. I didn't know how she was going to react but I was hoping that she would feel more at ease now that two of the most important things she had requested were either done or would be in a few hours. However, she did not even show a sign of excitement or relief; it was as though she was anticipating this move.

I asked her if it was okay for me to schedule a meeting with the Archbishop and his assistant to finalize our divorce and to also document our financial agreement on paper so that we could both be free to live our lives and, most importantly, it would give me time to schedule a flight for three, which was hard to do at that time.

Once she heard the news, and my request to move quickly with the divorce, she said in a sarcastic and calm tone, "We'll see."

To be honest with you, sweetheart, I felt like strangling her over the phone if I could have, just for the way she was talking to me. "What do you mean by, 'we'll see?'" I asked her. "We made a deal and I did as you asked. Your brother is meeting with my friend this afternoon and you will get your money. Now what else is there? We need to move on this quickly so I can get my travel arrangements handled before they try to attack the airport again."

I did not like where this was going and my blood was boiling with anger. I thought that if she backed off of our deal this time, I just didn't know what I would do. I was furious with the way she was taunting me and keeping me hanging.

She said that she would wait for her brother to call her after he received the money and once he hired a lawyer to inspect the court documents.

I didn't know what to say. I was dealing with someone who had no heart or feelings whatsoever towards me or my kids. *This is unbelievable*, I thought. I told her to go ahead and take another day to have her brother do what the hell he needed to do, but I swore to myself that if they jeopardized my chances of getting out of this country, it was going to be an all-out war.

I got off the phone and started to put things on paper. I needed to get organized. After that phone call, I really had my doubts that she would go through with our agreement and let me take you both with me. I wanted to call my lawyer and my friend and just reverse the whole idea, but I couldn't do it. What if she was telling the truth this time?

The day turned to night quicker than I wanted, but it gave me a chance to call my lawyer to see if he had mailed out the documents to her brother. I was told that he had and that they should get there the next morning. I expressed to the attorney some of my concerns regarding the incident that had taken place with your mother. He just said that it was too late to reverse anything at that point and that I should just be careful how I negotiated with her from then on.

I then called my friend to check if he had met with her brother. He told me that he had and that all was okay. He said that her brother came to see him and he had him sign an agreement that he had received money on behalf of your mother and then left. My friend asked me if everything was all right. I said yes and told him I would keep him updated.

The next morning I woke up anxious. Hopefully your mother would have contacted her brother and found everything I was telling her to be true and perhaps we could then schedule an appearance in front of the Archbishop. I wanted this to be over so that I could get back to Nessim with an answer before I lost the chance that I had been awaiting for two years.

In the back of my mind, I was going to go through with both plans. I knew that if I were to go with Nessim's plan and it worked, I would get to America with you and your sister and still have loose ends with your mother with regard to our marriage. I understood that getting us out was the most important thing, but I wanted to be a step ahead so that we could move on with our lives. And the less loose ends with your mother the better.

As usual, I was getting prepared to talk with your mother that day. I asked if she had a chance to talk to her brother; she said yes. I asked if he had received the money and the court documents; she said that he had. "Great, so I will call and set up a meeting with the Archbishop and get things going because my schedule is very tight," I told her. "And things are very bad in Homs. We need to finalize our divorce and get it registered."

She paused then began to put obstacles in the way again. She said that her brother was still consulting an attorney and that she was not sure if this was the right thing to do any more, that it was a big decision and I shouldn't rush her. I was thinking to myself as she was talking, *Did I fall for this shit again? Did she just make me lose the only ace that I was holding against her and now she is changing her mind? Hell no,* I thought.

And just as I finished that thought, she said, "I need more time to think about this before I agree to see the Archbishop."

This is where I totally lost it again. I was yelling so badly on the phone and cursing that it felt like I was in a different dimension completely. I'm not sure that I remember the whole incident because my blood pressure probably elevated to the maximum it could take without me passing out. I kept saying, "What the hell is wrong with you? I am giving you everything that you asked for and then some. You wanted money, you got it. You wanted me to dismiss the case against you, I did. I am agreeing to give you a divorce and the right to be in our girls' lives. What more do you want?"

She calmly and with no sense of remorse said, "I just want to make sure that I am comfortable financially if I decide to stay here in Syria."

"Is that all you care about? Don't you understand that you are putting your children's lives in danger every hour that they are here? Don't worry about money. If you need more, I will send you more on a monthly basis. Please, let's just get this done and over with," I pleaded. I was still not getting anything but sarcasm, so I just hung up. I was blind with rage and anger and the only thing I wanted to do was to call my two guards and see what damage they could cause on this wicked family. But for now I needed to call Nessim and give him the go ahead.

It was Wednesday afternoon when I called Nessim. I was somewhat calm but in a different state of mind. I felt like someone else entirely. I was not thinking with my heart this time. "Is the option still available to us?" I asked him.

"Yes," he said.

"What do I need to do?" I asked.

He said that I would have to drive to Damascus again and meet someone there the next morning. I asked him to send his driver over right away because I wanted to stay at a hotel that night to avoid the possibility of closed freeways the next day. He agreed and sent his driver to meet me.

I got all the documents ready again and we headed out. I did not notify my paid guards for this trip simply to protect Nessim and his contact. This time we had to take a more direct route through the city of Homs where fighting was fierce. The driver had to take care of other business for Nessim along the way.

Forever Numb

Desperately prying myself from a horrid death
Gasping for air and my body was numb
Deeper and deeper as I held my breath
I experienced a vision of what's to come
        I began to realize more than ever
        How insignificant my life might be
        Just when I thought I was strong and clever
        It took merely a dream to paralyze me
What if anything does this all mean?
And why in the month of May and not in June
Much I did not do and much I've not seen
Wouldn't you say that that is too soon?
        The more I asked, the more I was shown
        A time line of events came to my surprise
        Everything I've read and have ever known,
        Was now flashing before my eyes
Soon, disturbing images began to appear
Slowly with nineteen hundred and fourteen
My heart be still and trembling with fear
As I witness the horror never before seen
        Scream if you will, weep if you must, focus still
        A voice would say, seemingly familiar yet quaint
        Perhaps a knock at the door and I'd awake at will
        But rare is this, and privileged am I, no not now be still

Floating in a world, not of this world, but another
Humbled by its shear genius and magnificent power
Eloquently speaking and with authority like a mother
"No one knows the year, month, day or the hour"
                Seven eleven two thousand and eleven at seven eleven
                A messenger of the United Nations will make his mark
                He will make many promises with his hand to heaven
                Many will believe, many will follow, the world goes dark
Panic, disorder, illness, hunger death and disease
Wrath, greed, sloth, gluttony, envy, pride and lust
This will surely pass as many will pass or surcease
In the beginning, ashes to ashes and dust to dust.

Chapter 19

I was not thrilled to take that route through Homs, but my adrenalin was so high that I did not care. We encountered the usual mandatory stops along the way and soon we were on the main highway to Damascus. There was a freeway interchange that was sort of entangled and the signs were not clear to me. My driver knew what he was doing so I had no input in the matter. I was just looking out the window and hoping that we would have a safe trip.

Gunfire and mortar shells were heard along the highway but I could not tell how close or how far. As we made our way through this interchange we witnessed a large explosion up ahead about a mile or so that literally rocked our car. I could see a large cloud of fire and smoke and thought that we were possibly in trouble. There was no way to return, as we were on a highway with no exit in sight. My driver was very concerned and asked me to take cover as we slowly approached the dark smoke.

It was pretty frightening not knowing what we were about to enter. We wanted to stop, but that could prove worse. We decided to proceed forward with caution. Not much further and there it was: on the side of the road, a fuel tanker completely obliterated and two small cars next to it, also completely engulfed in flames and their parts spread all over the place. There was an exit just a few feet from the scene and we quickly took it and headed back in the opposite direction. We had no idea what had just taken place.

My driver said that he had heard that militant groups were targeting fuel trucks headed towards Damascus and shooting them with missiles from a distance. This was a very close call and we got lucky that we were not going a little faster; we would have been right in the middle of it.

I asked the driver to take me back home and told him that we would have to do it the next day early in the morning.

This incident gave me a few hours to think about things and I thanked God that we got home safely. Time was of the essence, however, and we had to make it to Damascus the next morning if we wanted the documents stamped and the restriction removed prior to Friday when every government agency was closed. We also risked possibly losing our opportunity with Nessim's contact.

I called the driver and asked him to arrange for another taxi driver who he trusted to accompany us the next morning. I told him that I wanted the other driver to keep about ten minutes in front of us on his own and to keep us informed in the event he encountered any trouble. I also called my guards this time to follow us and keep watch. This way, I felt safer. And more importantly, we would not miss our appointment.

I wanted to share this with someone close to me at the time because I truly felt overwhelmed. The only person I could trust and who would understand was my friend Jamal. I went over late that evening and had a drink with him and shared with him part of the plan, but I gave him limited information. I felt better getting some of the anger out and went back home to try to get some rest.

Although I was extremely angry with your mother, I still needed to have some dialogue with her regarding you and your sister. I needed to be calm so that she could at least feel at ease to have me see you when the right time came to make our escape.

I once again swallowed my pride and put aside my anger and called her the next day to make arrangements for me to see you. Because should this plan work the way I wanted, our attempt to leave was going to happen in the next two days. The plan was now simple. Once we got the documents signed and removed the travel restriction placed on you, we would get in a taxi and immediately head towards the Lebanese border with not a thought or a second to waste.

The next morning I awoke absolutely exhausted and felt like the world was on my shoulders. I made some coffee and was smoking a cigarette when I got a phone call from my two guards. They were running late. The taxi driver showed up and gave me the signal to go. I walked over to him and noticed that he had another driver parked behind him. These vehicles were not officially marked, 'Taxi,' like they should have been, but because of the danger that taxi drivers were facing, they had to get creative and conceal them as normal cars. I was told that many taxi drivers had been killed over the last year because they would stop for a potential customer and end up with a militant person who would kill them and take their car.

Just to be courteous, I asked the driver to come in and have some coffee, but I really just wanted to kill a few minutes until my guards made it and gave me the signal. I was a little nervous and wanted this day to be the day that I could finally just breathe. I got my signal and asked the two drivers to get ready.

This time is going to be different, I thought. *I've had my share of close calls and bad luck and all the bullshit I can take. Let's get the show on the road and get this done.*

The drive so far was good and our taxi driver, who was now about five kilometers ahead, was reporting good news. He informed us that he was talking with other taxi drivers who were currently on the way to Damascus who assured him there was no immediate danger. That made me feel good and also gave me an opportunity to talk to your mother and see if there was anything new regarding her decision.

In her mind, I'll bet that she thought she was still in control. She had no idea that whether or not she agreed to anything, my plan was going to work, with her or without her. The reason I was still talking with her was again simply to keep the peace so that it would be easier for me to see you and your sister without too much trouble and, in the process, if I could resolve our divorce issue, it would be a major plus for me in the future.

I asked how she was doing and if she wanted to talk about anything. She said that she had had time to think about things again and if I wanted to set up a meeting with the Archbishop, she was okay with that. I shook my head with disbelief.

She must have a multiple personality disorder or something, I thought. *One day she is evil and can't be reasoned with and the next day she wants to have a constructive dialogue.*

Even though I did not trust a word she was saying, I nonetheless agreed and told her that she was doing the right thing. I wanted to make the conversation short and hang up before she changed her mind again or before I accidentally said something the wrong way and sent her on a spiral.

I immediately called the Archbishop's assistant and asked him to please meet with me and your mother at his earliest convenience. He agreed but informed me that even with a mutual agreement with your mother, the Archbishop would have the final say and to prepare mentally for the possibility that he may not grant us the divorce. I told him that I had all the faith in the world in him and that I was prepared to make it worth his while. I would learn later that those words would cost me a bundle.

We were halfway to Damascus when my driver got a phone call from our other taxi driver. He told him that he was at a dead stop and there were military barricades everywhere. He told him that there had been a battle with the Syrian army and some rebels and there was nowhere to cross. There was only one way to get to our destination and the road we were on was it.

My driver looked very concerned about the news and told the other driver to just be careful and take cover. I later learned that the other driver was his brother. Once again we were faced with a major decision. Do we continue to Damascus and hope that things get better or do we go back and start from zero again?

It was frustrating, to say the least. While the driver could have done as I asked, I could not be selfish and put both of us in danger. At the same time this was the most important trip for me and I needed to get these documents signed. I was now faced with the biggest predicament thus far.

I decided to call Nessim for advice. I explained the situation to him and expressed that I was fully committed to this plan and I could not afford to lose this opportunity. He said that he would call me back in a few minutes.

Meanwhile I told my driver to pull over for a few minutes until I heard back from Nessim. I was not sure what my two guards were thinking at that point and I couldn't call them from the taxi. I stepped outside to smoke a cigarette and made a call to them. I told them that we were waiting for a phone call and to just hang tight.

Nessim called back after only five minutes and gave me the news I did not want to hear. He said that the violence was really bad in Damascus and that he had spoken with his contact. He said that I had two choices. One, I could go back to Homs and wait until Monday and try again or, two, I could drive to the city of Latakia where his contact had a friend who would be able to stamp our documents and also remove the travel restriction.

So there we were, on the side of the road, with a big decision to make. Latakia was completely in the opposite direction and, from what I gathered, would take us four hours to get there. And furthermore, the offices there closed at four o'clock.

I was not going to miss this opportunity, no matter what we had to do. I asked the driver if he would be okay with driving me to Latakia. He was very hesitant. He said that he had other obligations and even if he agreed, he added, there was no guarantee that the roads would be open to Latakia. I assured him that I would take care of him financially and informed him of how very important this was to me and my girls. He agreed and that same moment we turned around and headed in the opposite direction to Latakia.

It was now about 11am and we needed to move fast if we were to make it before the immigration offices closed. I had a great driver. He knew his way around the country and more importantly, I felt I could trust him. The long drive gave us a chance to talk about our families and I found that he was currently engaged to be married to his high school sweetheart and he was doing everything he could to make enough money to buy a house and start a family. He seemed very genuine and I like that about people.

The drive also served me well in that it gave me time to dig into my inner soul and try to go back to the person I really am. I guess situations can and do change people. I had no real intentions of hurting anyone. I felt normal about what I was doing and thought that I was only doing what any father would do to protect his kids and keep them safe. I was not committing an evil sin, I kept reminding myself. I began to make mental promises and reminders in the event everything went well and I was able to successfully make it to America with you and your sister.

I wanted, more than anything, to live a normal life, whatever that means. I wanted to wake up with both of you once again without looking at a watch. Take you to school without looking over my shoulder. I wanted to go to work and come home to read you a bedtime story and kiss you good night. I wanted you to have that sense of security of knowing that you are in your own home, your Daddy's home, and no one was going to take you away again.

For a long time I was asking that all-important question: why do people go through certain difficulties in their lives? There must be a reason beyond our own understanding. I guess that is something we will never know. Some people lose a child to an illness and ask why. Others lose their lives at a young or unexpected age. And yet others go through life not experiencing any major losses and are still miserable.

Right then, in my own life, I stopped asking questions and began to focus on my own actions. I was now okay with the theory that if my own conscience was at peace with a decision I make, then it was the right thing to do. Whether this theory is scientific or religious, I don't know. But at that point, it was what I was adopting.

Around 2:30 in the afternoon, we arrived in the beautiful city of Latakia. This was where your mother and I had spent our honeymoon and now where I was about to get our ticket to freedom.

Right away we asked for directions and found that we were about fifteen minutes away from the immigration building where we were to meet with our contact.

The city was calm for the most part. This was the city of the President and the majority there were Alawites and supporters of the President. We did not hear a single bullet go off. It was an eerie feeling, not hearing guns and mortar shots. I felt good about my decision to go there and was hopeful that things would work out.

We made our way into the building, and with some help, we got to the right office. We asked for the gentleman by name and he came out to greet us. I didn't know how much he knew about my situation, so I briefed him for a few minutes and handed him all the documents. He went over them pretty quickly and began to input the information into the computer. A minute later the electricity went out. I was caught off guard and didn't know what had just happened. *Not now,* I thought. *We are so close.*

The man asked me to go into the hallway that was now lit by way of a generator. "This is normal and there is nothing to worry about," he said. "The electricity goes off a couple times a day to save energy. But that is the least of your worries," he added.

"What is the problem?" I asked.

"The internet has been down all day," he told me, "and even if I could help you with all your documents, the travel restriction will not be lifted since it has to be activated via the internet."

"That is the most important thing and the reason I drove here today," I told him. I added that I intended to travel this weekend and I needed my daughters' names cleared at all borders if that was going to work.

He assured me that it would be okay. He said that he would do his job of signing and stamping the documents and while the office would be closed the next day, he would be there first thing on Saturday to make sure that the email went out to all border crossings to remove their names from restricted status to normal status.

I waited in the hallway for about thirty minutes until the electricity came back on. I approached the man's desk once again and stressed to him how important this was. He was so nice and comforting. He promised me that he would call me personally on Saturday morning and give me the green light to travel without a problem. I was on cloud nine once again.

I did it, I did it! Finally, freedom was in my grasp. I took a deep breath and thanked the man and told him that I would never forget what he and his friend did for me and my kids. I also invited him to my house if he ever made his way to America. What an incredible feeling I had as I asked my driver to take us to the most exclusive restaurant he knew. I said that I wanted it to have an oceanfront view. For some reason I just wanted to look at a horizon that had no border. And sure enough we ended up at a beautiful restaurant on the beach where I sat and stared at the endless waterfront.

Back at home safe and sound that same evening, I felt untouchable. What I had been working towards for the last two years was now a reality. In two days I would get the green light and then all I had to do was have access to you and your sister and off we would go.

It would have been Thursday morning in America that evening and I decided to call my travel agent to check on flight tickets for three. I had two choices to fly out of. I could fly directly out of Damascus International Airport since there would be no restrictions on any of us, or I could drive through the Lebanese border and fly out of Beirut. I did not want to risk being in Syria even for a day longer than necessary, just in case some freak thing happened and someone found out. So I asked for a flight out of Beirut. I was told that the next available flight to America was a week away. That meant I would have to cross the border and stay at a hotel until that date.

Many things were going on in my head. But the biggest concern was that if I got my chance to cross the border with you and your sister, would the Syrian authorities have jurisdiction in Lebanon to get you back if your mother was to report you missing? That was a major concern. However, if I waited in Syria until the flight date, drove directly to the airport and flew out immediately, chances were they would not have enough time to react and by then we would be in the air. That scenario was also dangerous because I would have to stay in the country for the seven days and possibly face criminal charges if we got caught.

At the moment I didn't have to make any decisions since I didn't have the green light any way, and I had a couple of days to see what developed with the Archbishop.

I awoke the next morning feeling like I was on top of the world. I was now in control for the most part. I was holding all the cards. I had possession of the real, valid passports, while she had no idea that she was holding invalid and canceled ones. I had all the necessary travel documents and by the following morning I would have the travel restriction removed. She had nothing on me whatsoever, other than she had you and your sister with her parents, which I would have no real problem with.

And as for the divorce thing, which was the least of my worries, it would have to be dealt with at a later time. I thought that now, at my leisure, I could talk with the Archbishop's assistant and see if he could get the divorce documents prepared, which would be the icing on the cake if it went through. And if it didn't, who cared. I could always have my attorney in America file for it.

I called and spoke with the assistant and asked him to prepare the documents and gave him instruction on how they should read. I told him to include the list of demands that your mother had asked for, including the money and visitation rights if she decided to go back to America. I also asked him to give me custody of you and your sister for the duration of my stay in Syria. He said that your mother would never agree to that.

"Just try it," I said. "You never know, especially as she is now getting everything she asked for."

He laughed and said okay.

I called your mother and told her that I had spoken with the Archbishop's office and had given them instructions to proceed with what we both had agreed to and that, hopefully, by tomorrow, the assistant would have a rough copy for us to approve. She was happy to hear that and did not show a change of heart at that point.

I asked her if I could pick up you and your sister the next morning, which would be Saturday morning. She agreed. I must admit that I was elated that everything was going so smoothly thus far and that by tomorrow morning I would know our fate once I heard from my man in Latakia. For the remainder of the day, I decided to make my final rounds around the village and see family and friends and say my silent goodbyes.

My sister Miriam, who had played such a big role in keeping me positive and grounded, was someone I was going to miss dearly. She noticed my mood right away. She said that I looked like the cat that swallowed the canary. I smiled and just gave her a hug. I didn't want to tell her everything yet, but I told her that I had a good feeling that this time around, I would not be leaving the country alone. She just smiled and looked to the heavens, saying, *"Inshalla"* (God willing).

Dust in the Wind

The sword of vengeance is not satisfied with enough bloodshed.
Nor is the sea quenched with all the rivers it's fed.
And when does a fire say enough, as long as there is a weed?
Or a man, find contentment in his veracious appetite for greed?
If you are to strive for worldly things, best be
prepared for the disaster it brings.
King Solomon knew best, and once had it all
All his heart's desires, at his beck and call.
He had riches and fame like none before.
But this emptiness, he wanted to explore.
He built for himself castles with the rarest of stone
He gathered silver and gold and treasures unknown.
He had maidens and servants and chariots galore
And created great works for people to adore.
Seeking knowledge and wisdom, short of insanity;
Vanity of vanities, all is vanity.
He preached day and night, for everyone to hear it.
In the conclusion, it is vexation of the spirit.
We are but dust in the wind, and the end is at hand.
But the word of the Almighty will forever stand.

Chapter 20

Saturday morning couldn't come early enough. I awoke at dawn. I looked outside and it was a beautiful summer day with a little haze covering the hundreds of acres of vineyards and almond fields. I made a cup of coffee and decided to take a stroll. I lit a cigarette and walked down a dirt path that literally was the color of blood. This village had been blessed with good soil and they were famous for producing fine almonds and great grapes to brew Arak Liquor. *I will miss this,* I thought. I was at peace within myself and sort of felt in my heart that things would work out.

At around nine that morning I received the phone call I had been waiting for. It was the gentleman from the immigration office. I could hardly take a breath just waiting for some good news.

"Congratulations," he said, "your paperwork is completed and the travel restrictions on your daughters have been lifted." It was an incredible feeling of relief and I couldn't stop thanking him. He said that rather than put a time frame on the restriction, he removed it indefinitely.

I hung up with him and got ready to go to Alhafar to pick up you and your sister. That would be one of the most memorable days thus far. My patience and tenacity, and the help of so many good friends and relatives, had finally paid off. While I was there in Alhafar, I paid a visit to my dear cousin Zouhair to whom I owe a big debt of gratitude. He is someone I will never forget.

I wasn't sure what I was going to do when I finally had you both in my car. A lot of ideas were spinning in my head. But I wanted to be sure and not rush into anything. The best thing to do, I thought, was to just take you home to my village and figure things out more rationally.

The drive back to my village was unlike any other time. I felt like I had options that were not afforded to me before. I could literally just drive to the border with no thought in the world. But again I kept a level head and continued driving home. While you and your sister played, I began to pack my bags. I wasn't sure whether I was going to just pick you up and drive to Damascus without telling anyone or just wait to see what developed with the Archbishop.

This was a very sensitive time. Anything could happen. Your mother could have another change of heart and throw this whole thing out of control by taking you to Damascus and I wouldn't know how to get to you. Or your grandparents could have already purchased airline tickets for you and your sister to travel with them to Guatemala. Or a computer glitch could happen and all of my hard work could vanish. I had to make a decision.

I called the pastor to see if he had finished preparing the documents. He said that he had, and if I wanted to, I could meet with him and the Archbishop the next afternoon after church services. I told him that I would call your mother to see if that would work for her and get back with him.

I called your mother and asked her if she could make it the next afternoon. She said she could and that she would be accompanied by her uncle. I said that was no problem and then called the pastor back to confirm. The pastor asked me to meet with him in private an hour before the arranged meeting. I kind of knew what it was about, but I did not speculate and I obliged his request. I asked him what would happen if your mother changed her mind at the last minute like she had done before. He assured me that if she did that this time, she would lose all credibility with the Archbishop and that would shift everything in my favor. He said that the Archbishop was not one to mess with and it would be unwise on her part.

As I hung up the phone with the pastor, my mind began to wonder. I thought, *Why do I need to subject myself to her drama, selfish demands and all the money she is asking for.* I could just get into a car, take you and your sister; drive to the Lebanese border and just take off to America. And if your mother was brave enough to go face the consequences of child abduction charges, blackmail and extortion, by all means let her. Because that is exactly what she had done. She had extorted money and blackmailed me to drop the lawsuit against her in America in exchange for the release of my girls. The more I sat there and thought of it, the more I just wanted to do it.

My head was filled with images of the last two years and all the heartache your mother and her family had put me and you through. The lonely nights that I would come home to an empty house burning for a kiss or a hug from you and your sister. The sleepless nights I would endure thinking about the bombings taking place outside your windows in Homs. The embarrassment, betrayal and difficulties your mother put me through and the destruction of a family.

All of these thoughts made me nauseous and I wanted more than anything to erase them from my memory. A human being is capable of many unthinkable acts, but for your mother to be reduced to this low level was not only a disappointment to me, but to the many friends and family members who loved her, as well.

Unfortunately, she was still the mother of my children and for your sake and your sister's sake, I would not let her change who I am. I would not give her the satisfaction of saying that I ran off and left her to fend for herself. I would not treat her as she treated me. And most importantly, I would not take for granted the grace of God that was shown to me.

After much of this painful thinking, my conscience kicked in and I decided to do the right thing. I had come this far and I still had the option of leaving at any time, so why not just wait another day and see if she was going to go through with it. Worst case scenario, I would be out several thousands of dollars to her and whatever financial contributions I had to forfeit to the Archbishop fund. This way my conscience would be clear and the divorce would be final. And if she completely changed her mind and decided to pull any funny business, I was more than prepared this time around, to the point of no mercy.

At this point, I did not have a scheduled flight because I wasn't sure where I was flying out of or whether there would still be an airport in operation in Damascus. But the Lebanese border was always the clear choice. I left you and your sister in Alfouhila with my sister and drove alone to Fairouzeh to meet with the pastor, and soon after, we were scheduled to meet with the Archbishop.

Before signing any documents, your mother had to have enough money in hand, other than the money that her brother had received in

America. So I was prepared for that. But I was not prepared for the surprise amount of money that was asked of me by the pastor as his fee and the fee of more prominent people involved in this case, including the Archbishop.

As the pastor got into my car, he asked me to drive him away from the church to a more discrete location where we had some privacy to discuss the way this whole case would go down. We ended up in some alley where he felt comfortable. I could tell that he was about to give a speech. He began by telling me about the normal divorce procedure for Syriac Orthodox Christians. He said that it was a lengthy and costly process and it often could take up to seven years.

"However," he continued, "we know how sensitive your situation is, with the war going on in the country, and we understand that it has been difficult for you and the children being thousands of miles apart."

Where is he going with this story? Get to the point already, I thought to myself.

He said that after the hundreds of cases he had overseen in the past forty years, this case was the most complex and difficult case thus far. He said that he knew your mother was lying about many things and that he understood why. He said that most women who seek a divorce usually lie about being beaten or abused and even go so far as to say their husband was unfaithful.

He said that he knew from the first day he met me that I was a good-hearted man and was telling the truth. Furthermore, he had called other pastors in the congregation in America to check on my character as the hearings were taking place and was convinced I had been a good father and husband and was in good standing with the church in America.

What a speech, I thought. I just thanked him for his faith in me and waited for the request.

He looked me in the eye and said, "I don't want you to think that we are demanding anything from you, like terrorists," he laughed, "but, as you know, things in the country have been very dangerous and money has been very tight."

I stopped him and said, "I understand. What can I do for you?"

He said that his son was attending college and that he really needed much financial help, and with a pastor's salary, it was almost impossible to provide for him.

My heart was pounding when I heard that. Was this guy asking me to pay for his son's college tuition? "Whatever I can do to help," I said again. "Please, just let me know. After all, you are helping me a great deal."

He named the amount he wanted and said that it would cover all fees to him and the Archbishop, as well as all filing fees. While I was disgusted with the amount, I was more so with the tactic he was using to extract as much as possible, knowing my vulnerable and sensitive situation. Bribery is a normal practice in this country and probably in most countries. But when it starts playing a role in the church, it is simply despicable.

I smiled and agreed to do it but only after your mother had signed and agreed to all the terms. We returned to the church to meet with the Archbishop and I hoped that your mother and her uncle were already there.

We got to the church and waited for the Archbishop to get off his throne and come down to finish our business. By then I just wanted this shit to be over. I could have cared less about the corrupt or the faithful, no offense. I just wanted to get on a plane and get the hell out of that place.

Moments later your mother and her uncle showed up, as did the Archbishop, himself. I did not pay him the normal respect, which is to bow down your head as you approach him. I simply extended my hand. I sat across from your mother and her uncle as the pastor prepared the documents for all of us to sign. There was not much emotion shown from either one of us. It felt like we were conducting a normal business deal.

The pastor presented the documents to your mother and she handed them to her uncle to inspect. They were written in Arabic but translated to English so that I could understand them. I also read them and agreed. She objected to the part where you and your sister would now be in my custody, but the pastor immediately jumped in and told her that it was a formality since the father needed to arrange for their flight. She did not say anything more.

We were handed a couple of pens and I couldn't sign fast enough. Your mother also signed and I could not help but notice the silence in the room. No one had anything to say. I just looked at your mother and with a little sarcasm said, "Wow, ten years of marriage dissolved in ten minutes, congratulations."

The Archbishop asked the pastor to call someone at the immigration office to arrange for the removal of the travel restriction on you and your sister and instructed him to then fax the approval over to them. My heart just about fell to my stomach. I knew that if they called and found the restriction had already been removed, the situation was going to get very ugly, very fast.

Without raising suspicion, I asked the pastor if it was okay for me to just take the document there personally so that way there was no possibility of it getting lost. "You know how chaotic things are," I said jokingly. He smiled and agreed to give it to me. *That was a close call,* I thought.

As I concluded my business with all involved, I could not wait to get home and call my travel agent in America. *Did this just happen?* I kept asking myself. *I can't believe that everything went my way. I've got my girls, I've got my divorce and in a couple days I will be in America celebrating with my family and friends.*

On the way back to my village, I cried the whole way there. I felt so light, as though something heavy had been lifted off my shoulders. Finally, I could put this nightmare behind me and start my life all over again.

No sooner did I get home than your mother called and asked me if it was okay for her to take you and your sister back to Alhafar so that you could say goodbye to her family and your school friends. I thought about it for a second and smiled to myself. This was a nice feeling; your mother was now asking my permission to see you. I told her that it would be fine, but because of the problems with the airport, I needed you back the next day so that I could have enough time to drive to Damascus before any road closures. She agreed and then came by the same day to pick you up.

I hope I am not making a mistake, I thought. *Your mother has now gotten everything she requested. Money, divorce, free of the case in America, and the right to see and be with you. What would stop her from fleeing with you again?* Nonetheless, I still took a chance.

That night I called my travel agent and booked the first flight out of Syria. It would be in three days. I packed my bags and decided to visit with my sisters and their families. I told them that your mother and I had come to an agreement and that she was allowing me to take you and your sister back to America. They could not believe it; they thought that I was kidding.

For your sake, I told everyone that your mother was concerned about her children's safety and decided that it would be best if they were back in America. I decided not to share the ugly and manipulative side of your mother and how I had arrived at that conclusion. At first, the reaction I got was disbelief. They told me that she might have played me for a fool once again, just to get her way. They told me that, as your mother, she could change her mind at the last second and have any police stop me at the airport. I told them that I had an agreement signed by the Archbishop. But they insisted that she could still change her mind and to be very careful.

I went back home that evening kind of disappointed in myself and began to blame myself for allowing her to take you back even for a day. I couldn't wait until the next morning to see if she was, in fact, going to bring you back.

The next morning I called to talk with you and check up on the situation. I spoke with your mother and stressed to her that I needed to get to Damascus immediately so that I could take care of some documents for you and your sister and that they needed you to be present. She was a little suspicious but agreed to have you back that afternoon.

There was no time to waste. I called my trusted taxi driver and asked him to drive us to Damascus and to do the same thing as we had before, to bring another driver with him to drive in front of us and to be at my house as soon as possible. This time I would not be taking any more chances. I called my two guards and told them that I needed them to meet me at the house that afternoon so that they could play their last role and get paid the rest of their money.

Everything was now in motion; the only thing left was for your mother to show up on time. I had my sisters there, along with some friends, saying their final good byes as your mother pulled up with you, your sister and your grandparents. They did not want to come into the house, which was just fine with me. My driver also showed up at that time and we began to load our bags into his taxi. He had brought over his brother again, which made me feel good that he was still alive and well.

I couldn't wait to get into the taxi with you and just drive away. After some hugs and kisses and a lot of tears, I put you and your sister into the taxi and we were ready to go.

Your grandfather asked if he could have a word with me. I obliged. He asked if I would allow you and your sister to contact him and your grandmother once we made it to America and he was very apologetic about what they had put me through. In my mind I was thinking just the opposite. I didn't want you and your sister to ever have contact with anyone in that family, but I promised him that I would allow you to contact them.

I got into the taxi and we headed towards Damascus. *At last, we are really going home this time,* I thought to myself.

As soon as we got on that highway, I felt at ease. I had no particular hotel lined up when we reached Damascus, but I was sure there would not be a shortage of hotels once we got there. I wanted to be at a hotel that was very close to the airport because, for the last few days, we had been hearing that the main highway to the airport had been the center of fighting with rebels and the Syrian army. So I called the hotel that was a block away from the airport to reserve a room but found that the hotel was now occupied by foreign visitors and was off limits to the general public.

After thinking things through for a little, I decided to call my old friend, Sam, and stay at his house and arrange for a taxi to drive us to the airport the next day. I told him about my situation and asked if we could crash at his place for the night. Of course he agreed and was happy to do it. I had not seen him since the last time we had hidden out at his place, a year and a half earlier, when I had taken you and your sister to the U.S. Embassy.

Things were good and we did not encounter much gunfire on the highway. However, once we got to Damascus, things were different. Driving through the narrow streets just to get to my friend's house was an ordeal. There was panic in the air and gunfire was loud and clear. I just couldn't wait to get there safely and to fly out the next day.

Once we arrived, we unloaded our bags and brought them inside the house. I left you and your sister with my friend and excused myself for a few minutes. I wanted to thank the taxi driver and his brother and also to thank my two guards and pay them the rest of their money.

As they all took off, I just walked inside the house but still felt uneasy. I felt like I was on the run again. *When is this finally going to end and see us all on an airplane?* I thought.

I put you and your sister to bed and came downstairs to unwind and plan for the next morning. I asked Sam to arrange for a taxi to be waiting for us in the morning. We agreed that we would leave his house by ten the next morning and that way we could be at the airport about two hours early. If it was up to me, I would have liked to sleep on some bench inside the airport and wait for the flight just because I was so worried something might happen.

My phone rang and I could see on the screen that it was your mother. I ignored it. I didn't want to hear anything from her, good or bad. A few minutes later, another phone call. This time it registered your grandparents' home number. I again ignored it. *What is going on here? Did she have a change of heart again and is trying to find out where we are?* I was panicking all over again. I decided to shut my phone off all together and just try to go to sleep. I squeezed my way into your bed and held you tight until I fell asleep from total mental exhaustion.

The next morning I woke you and your sister up and got you ready with some comfortable clothes. I asked Sam to check on the taxi situation as I turned my phone on. I could see that there was a ton of missed calls, mostly from your mother. Again I dismissed them and continued to get ready.

At ten o'clock that morning, a taxi driver knocked on the door and we began to load our bags into the taxi. I gave the driver instructions to meet us at the airport while we drove behind him in my friend Sam's car. My phone rang, and sure enough, it was your mother. I answered this time, just to see what she wanted.

"Where are you?" she asked.

"We are just taking care of some final paperwork and heading to the airport immediately afterwards," I told her.

She said that she wanted to see you and your sister again and say goodbye. I did not have a good feeling about that. I told her that we didn't have time to wait.

She told me that she had driven to Damascus the night before and had tried to call me all night so that she could see you.

I lied and said that my phone had died and I did not get any calls.

She said that was fine, but she insisted on seeing you before we flew out.

I told her to meet us at the airport in one hour. We were about thirty minutes from the airport and I thought that if we could get there first and go through check in, there would be no way for her to cause any problems since she would not be able to go in without a flight ticket; there we would be safe. I told everyone to hurry and get to the airport right away. Sam told me to calm down and not to worry, that we had plenty of time before our flight left.

I had to tell him about the predicament I was in. He understood and immediately gunned the car to make it to the airport as soon as possible. Perhaps I was overreacting, but I didn't want to take any chances.

The drive to the airport was hectic and in the heat of the moment we lost our taxi driver. He had all of our bags and here we were trying to find his taxi among hundreds of similar taxis. I began to think if there was anything in our bags that I needed to make our flight.

I was holding my carry-on and I had all my documents with me, so I told Sam that if we didn't find the taxi driver in time, to just keep the bags and have them shipped to me later. I did not want to waste a single minute trying to find him or wait for him. I just wanted to get to the airport door before your mother got there and possibly hinder our departure.

As we approached the airport, we were stopped for inspection. The man who stopped us checked my passport and ID, and once he found me to be American, he wanted to talk about politics. I tried so hard to just end the conversation so we could make it to the airport on time. Finally, he returned my passport and ID and we headed towards the entrance of the airport.

That is when my friend noticed our taxi driver and motioned for him to meet us. I was yelling at everyone to hurry up and just get inside the terminal. I was looking all around me to see if your mother had made it already. I called for baggage handlers who were close by and asked them to rush our luggage inside.

As we got to the main entrance, I found that they were now checking passenger's bags before anyone could enter the terminal. So we were still outside the terminal and I was wondering if your mother had already arrived. The baggage check took forever, it seemed. I was holding on to your hand so tightly and was acting like I was in a hurry. And because of that, the guy began to ask more questions. I was getting so frustrated with him, because all I wanted to do was get to the point where only passengers could enter.

At last the man was satisfied and we rushed towards the "Passengers Only" gate. I kept looking to see if your mother was anywhere in sight while this other man was inspecting our tickets and passports. And then, in a matter of one second, we entered the door and I felt safe that from there on out; only passengers could enter. No more fear of your mother causing any trouble.

I proceeded to the check-in window and began to feel the stress of something possibly going wrong. I was praying that the travel restriction had been lifted and that there were no glitches. I was very nervous as I handed the girl our passports. She checked our luggage, gave me our boarding passes, and asked me to proceed to the proper gate.

This is too easy, I thought. If there was anything wrong, surely she would have said something. There was only one other window we would have to go through and we would be home free. I approached the final window and handed a man our passports. He asked a few questions, handed them back and said, "Have a nice flight."

I should have been relaxed at that point, but I was not. I wasn't going to relax until that flight was completely off the ground and far away. I was very anxious and wanted out of this country very badly. We had a couple of hours to kill, so we did some shopping at the many shops there.

I decided to get to our gate and wait there. It gave me the sense that we were closer to leaving. Moments later, passengers were being loaded onto the plane. I am not sure why I wanted us to be the last passengers rather that the first, but that is what happened.

Once the last person was checked in, I grabbed you and your sister's hands and walked towards the lady. It felt like everything was in slow motion, like it was a dream. I felt numb and could barely hear anything clearly. I was looking at the lady tear off the stub on my boarding pass and the tear sounded muffled. But I could also hear my name being called out. Was I going insane or what? I know I heard my name but the lady's lips were not moving. It felt so surreal. And in a split second I realized that the sound was coming from someone who was standing right behind me that I did not even know was there.

In a panic I quickly turned around. "Are you Alex?" a young lady asked.

"Who are you and what do you want?" I answered back with a mean tone and a frightening stare.

She was startled and almost fell backwards. She stuttered and said, "A lady asked me to find you and tell you that she wanted to say goodbye to her kids."

With my teeth clinched, I said, "That ain't gonna happen!" I shoved you and your sister down the tunnel and kept walking.

Once on the plane, I was looking outside the window to see if it was going to be surrounded by flashing lights from police cars as if I was in some movie. The waiting time before takeoff was torture. I could not wait to get the hell out of the country. The engine sound was like music to my ears, and once the wheels began to roll back, my heart sang with joy.

And then we began moving forward, faster and faster. I crossed my heart as I felt the wheels leave the ground. We were free at last!

I looked at both of you sitting next to me and could not believe that we had finally made it. We were on our way back home to America. Thank you, Lord.

Epilogue

Our new life in America

Looking back just a couple of years ago, no one thought that this was even possible. I had begun to accept the idea of being away from my two little girls until they each reached the age of eighteen.

In retrospect it is easier for one to look at one's life in chapters rather than days gone by and say that this incident or that trial was simply a chapter in the many chapters of our lives. I believe that while we do get to write our own words in each chapter, we do not get to choose the titles.

Earning the title "Single Dad with Two Children" never sounded so good. I had that feeling as our plane touched the ground at LAX airport on July 25, 2012.

I did not have a plan or any idea of how I was going to successfully raise two little girls on my own. All I cared about that day was that my two girls were finally home.

As we drove down the 105 Freeway headed home, I couldn't help but look at the tall buildings and how everything around me was intact. My heart was an emotional wreck as images of destroyed buildings and streets covered in ruble filled my mind. It's hard to explain the feeling of going from a country at war to a country at peace within twenty-four hours.

Pulling up the driveway of our house was both emotional and surreal. The anxious feeling of being on the run did not subside until I actually took my girls inside and closed the door. Once inside, I felt an amazing feeling of peace come upon me. I looked at my girls roaming the house as though they had never left.

Our life today is no different than most people. And my life as a single dad is no different than most single dads. I hired a nanny to take care of my children while I went back to work at the same dealership. While I have no time for a personal life, I love waking up in the morning and preparing breakfast for my girls and getting them ready for school. And I love coming home to find my children waiting for me.

I have been blessed with a most supportive and caring family. As for my girls, they are enrolled in school and are doing very well, adjusting to their new life. They are surrounded by family and cousins who love them very much. As of today, they are six and nine years of age.

They don't talk of the time spent in Syria very much, but the nightmares they both have at least two or three times a week are a constant reminder of those ugly days. I just hold them and assure them that everything will be okay.

As for their mother, she fled Syria and temporarily moved back to America. In 2013 the court granted me full custody of my two girls with only supervised visits with their mother. On my terms.

About the Author

Zavian Escandar is an immigrant born in Homs, Syria. He moved to the United States with his family at the age of ten. After graduating High School, he began to work with his father in the family business. As he became of age, he began to explore with different business ventures and also became interested in the field of inventions.

Zavian currently lives and works in Southern California. He is the proud father of two beautiful girls who are nine and six years of age. He enjoys golf, tennis, reading, writing and the great outdoors. While he does not consider himself a dedicated author, he is currently working on a second book "Our Father Who Art In Heaven". For more information about the author, visit www.zavianescandar.com